Money With a Mission

Money With a Mission

by
Dr. Leroy Thompson Sr.

Harrison House
Tulsa, Oklahoma

Unless otherwise indicated, all Scripture quotations are taken from the *King James Version* of the Bible.

Direct quotations from the Bible appear in bold type.

Money With a Mission
ISBN 1-57794-345-7
Copyright © 2000 by Dr. Leroy Thompson Sr.
Ever Increasing Word Ministries
P.O. Box 7
Darrow, Louisiana 70725

Published by Harrison House, Inc.
P.O. Box 35035
Tulsa, Oklahoma 74153

Contents

In this book, I'm going to talk about divine prosperity in a way that is beyond houses, cars, clothes, jewelry, and bank accounts. Yet if you pay attention to the Spirit of God and follow godly instruction, what I'm teaching can take care of all your financial shortages, problems, and dilemmas. You will never struggle about money again. You can put on the garment of deliverance and trade in your garment of lack and striving in your own self to try to get ahead or to make something happen for yourself financially.

However, I cannot talk about money, and divine prosperity in particular, without talking first about faith. In order to receive anything from God, including money, you have to use faith. You don't receive by feeling or emotion. You grasp the things of God with your spirit—your mind cannot grasp them. And you believe with your spirit—your heart, or inner man—not with your mind.

So the things I share in this book, I encourage you to study using the Word of God. Pay close attention to what the Holy Spirit tells you in your spirit. And be faithful to act on what you've learned, for it's putting faith and the Word of God into practice that effects a cure, brings deliverance, changes a life and even transforms a nation.

An Important Phrase

A phrase I want you to remember and contemplate is "money with a mission." You will be seeing that phrase again and again as I open the Word to you concerning money's mission. If you truly get hooked up with money's mission according to the Word of God, you will prosper and succeed in life, and God's work will prosper. It will be accomplished in the earth, and it will be accomplished quickly. Gone will be the days of ministers or ministries having to wait ten or fifteen years to do what God has given them to do. They'll do it tomorrow. Why? Because believers are going to give them the money to do it.

I was ministering in Chicago when God dropped these two words in my spirit: Money Missionaries. (Don't let those words become mundane to you, because within them is the power to change your life. Those words may be just words, but they are a vehicle to carry the divine.)

As long as I've been teaching on divine prosperity as my commission from God, I never heard these two words in connection with the subject until God dropped them in my spirit that night in Chicago. As soon as I heard them, I fully understood what they meant.

God has called every one of His children, not just a few, to be money missionaries. Now what do I mean by that? Every single one of God's children should be handling money for Him—on His behalf in the earth realm, doing what He tells them to do, when He tells them to do it, and how He tells them to do it.

Why are we called to be money missionaries? It's because we are to bring the Kingdom of God into manifestation to man. In other words, we are to use our money in exchange for souls!

So our main objective in handling money for God is to yield it to Him for the sake of souls. When I say "handling money for God," I'm talking about handling our money. We are to yield our money to Him to use as a money missionary, so to speak. The money you have is money that has been given to you to carry out the mission on earth that all men might come to the saving knowledge of the Lord Jesus Christ. In fact, I'll give you the secret to financial success in a nutshell: When your money becomes a "missionary," having the elementary material aspects of prosperity (houses, cars or whatever you desire) will become no problem for you.

When your motives concerning money are right, when you have a heart for souls and the advancement of God's Kingdom and you yield yourself and your money to God as a money missionary, God knows then that He can trust you. He knows that you will remain focused on money's main purpose, and His desire will be seeing that more money gets into your hands.

Money for Souls

As I said in the introduction, every single one of us is called to be a money missionary—to allow our money to be used for His mission. Once you answer that call individually, or personally, you have to slap doubt out of the way. And the information I'm going to arm you with in this book will give you the power to do it! You can slap doubt away with God's prophetic word "money missionaries."

You see, when you are convinced of God's mission, or purpose, for money, then you will not be distracted. You know you are on the right track. You can say, "I am in agreement with God and His will concerning money. I am going to yield my money to Him, and I am going to prosper as a result. Nothing can stop me—no man, no demon, no hindrance or obstacle. I am a money missionary!"

As a money missionary, you are putting yourself in a position for God to pack your account with money.

Someone may say, "Well, that doesn't sound right. That sounds like 'pie in the sky.'" But as you yield your money to God in faith, you are telling Him, "I know how to handle money. Money is not going to be my master. I am going to master money for You in the earth's realm." And let me tell you, there is nothing God won't do for you! There is nothing God won't do for any one of His money missionaries.

Now, the idea of yielding your money to God and being a money missionary might not excite you. But it should, because it is the key to your never having a money problem another day in your life.

The Lord told me, *Tell the people to receive My call*. I encourage you to receive the call and to forget about houses, cars, clothes and so forth. If you will answer God's call, you can have so many clothes that you can't possibly wear them all! But God wants you to have your priorities straight.

The World Is Not Our Home!

The reality is that we have been left in this earth's realm, not to put up a permanent dwelling place—not to get caught up in the mundane, everyday affairs of life. We are going to have to leave here one day. So while we're here, we want to finish our assignment from God, not seek our own pleasure and comfort.

Our assignment is to finish what the Lord Jesus Christ started when He was here. He was here to redeem mankind—to purchase us and to bring us back to God. Well, He purchased us with His own blood and has legally brought us back to God. He has broken down the wall that separated us from our Creator. The Bible says that God is not holding men's trespasses against them.

So now we must reconcile man to God, because the price has been paid. We must herald the Good News and tell the world that it is finished! We must tell them that the price has been paid, the work has been done. Certainly, we are to do that one-on-one and be witnesses and lights in our own worlds—our neighborhoods and communities. But, largely, it's going to take money to fund the spreading of the Gospel across the globe.

Being a money missionary means that you are passing out money to further God's Kingdom. You are excited when you get money in your hands, because that means you can pass out some more money. You buy a car every now and then, but it's no big deal as you continue to pass out money. The cars don't mean anything to you. In fact, you can see someone without a car and say, "Hey, come here. You don't have to walk anymore. Here." And you give that person a car!

Money has lost its hold on you. Material things have lost their hold. You are a money missionary for the Kingdom of God. People will say, "He is wild! He's crazy! He loves to give money away!" But you're not crazy. You are a money missionary, and the only meaning that money has to you now is how to reach more people. You are sort of like an addict. You wake up in the morning and say, "Where can I give next? Lord, what do You want me to do now?" because you just have to give some money away.

Wasted Goods

Read carefully the following account of a steward who wasted his master's goods.

And he said also unto his disciples, There was a certain rich man, which had a steward;

and the same was accused unto him that he had wasted his goods.

And he called him, and said unto him, How is it that I hear this of thee? give an account of thy stewardship; for thou mayest be no longer steward.

Then the steward said within himself, What shall I do? for my lord taketh away from me the stewardship: I cannot dig; to beg I am ashamed.

I am resolved what to do, that, when I am put out of the stewardship, they may receive me into their houses.

So he called every one of his lord's debtors unto him, and said unto the first, How much owest thou unto my lord?

And he said, An hundred measures of oil. And he said unto him, Take thy bill, and sit down quickly, and write fifty.

Then said he to another, And how much owest thou? And he said, An hundred measures of wheat. And he said unto him, Take thy bill, and write fourscore.

And the lord commended the unjust steward, because he had done wisely: for the children of this world are in their generation wiser than the children of light.

And I say unto you, Make to yourselves friends of the mammon of unrighteousness; that, when ye fail, they may receive you into everlasting habitations.

He that is faithful in that which is least is faithful also in much: and he that is unjust in the least is unjust also in much.

If therefore ye have not been faithful in the unrighteous mammon, who will commit to your trust the true riches?

And if ye have not been faithful in that which is another man's, who shall give you that which is your own?

No servant can serve two masters: for either he will hate the one, and love the other; or else he will hold to the one, and despise the other. Ye cannot serve God and mammon.

Luke 16:1-13

Please pay close attention to the phrase "wasted his goods" because it is very important. Until you understand the call that you have on your life in the area of financial management, you are going to waste the Lord's goods. When you waste what He gives to you, He can't afford to give you much more, because you haven't grown enough yet to know how to handle it properly. Many in the Body of Christ today waste the Lord's goods. That is a sad indictment, but even many of those who have received the call to be money missionaries have not been sensitive enough to the call and to the Lord's leading. They've gotten sidetracked on other things and have lost sight of the primary purpose for their money.

The primary call that is on all of our lives is to see to it that not one man, one woman, one boy or one girl goes to hell because we held back a dollar. Are you wasting any money? Are you using your money trying to get what you want in life? God is going to make sure you get what you want—but only if you will give Him what He wants.

This is not just a nice Sunday school lesson. This is the very lesson that is going to bring you into finances like you've never seen before. So stop wasting what you have and use it for the glory of God.

Why No Breakthrough? Check Your Stewardship

And he called him, and said unto him, How is it that I hear this of thee? give an account of thy stewardship; for thou mayest be no longer steward.

Luke 16:2

Some in the Body of Christ used to be stewards—money missionaries—but they're not anymore. They have raggedly and irresponsibly handled what God has given them. But they can come back. God is waiting for them to repent and change their ways and their relationship with money before He can take them further with stewardship.

You might be wondering yourself, *What is the problem? I love God, and I'm praying. I'm not committing adultery or living in sin. I'm tithing. Why don't I get my financial breakthrough?*

Your breakthrough is waiting for you on the other side of your stewardship. But your stewardship might be on hold. If so, you are going to have to give an account and repent. Then God will release your stewardship again. You still qualify for stewardship because you're in the Kingdom of God. But before you can continue with your assignment, you need to give an account as to why you didn't do what He wanted you to do with what He entrusted to you.

I'm telling you, we as the Body of Christ are on the verge of the biggest money explosion that ever existed in the history of mankind. We are on the verge of turning the key of wealth transference so that the world's wealth gets in the hands of Christians like never before. And I believe the concept of being a money missionary is the key to tapping into that wealth.

So check up on your stewardship. Some people think they're doing good, but they're not doing what they could and should be doing. They've settled into their giving routine. But, you see, it's not a regimen; it's a revelation. And when you see the light of what God wants for you and what He wants you to do for Him, you might find you aren't doing as well as you thought you were doing.

Let me say this: You can't prosper on someone else's revelation. You can't see someone else do something and then copy what he or she is doing. But you can seek God and let Him reveal to you day by day or season by season what your stewardship is to consist of. You can't think it up or make it up. You have to let God tell your heart, your spirit, what you are supposed to be doing as a money missionary.

As a money missionary, you are putting the devil on notice—and Heaven will back you—that you are going to be receiving bigger checks than the little checks you've been receiving just by doing things your own way. You are going to start handling checks from God, and checks from God are supernatural, overwhelming and overflowing! They just keep coming!

Repent and Be Sensitive

The Lord told me to say, "Check out your stewardship, repent and be sensitive." You know, we have to be sensitive to God to give when He wants us to, but we also have to be sensitive not to give when man is putting pressure on us.

Don't let anyone "prostitute" your money by taking it from you to use it incorrectly. Don't let someone just give a good talk and talk you into giving away all your money. Be sensitive; have some spiritual discernment. If

God is not moving, don't you move. It doesn't matter how good a minister might sound. If God's not in it, that minister doesn't have your best interest at heart, and that is not God's way. God doesn't take money from you to leave you with less. He always gives back. (See Luke 6:38; 2 Corinthians 9:6; and Galatians 6:7.) You can't out-give God!

Characteristics of a Good Steward

What are some of the characteristics of a good steward? Well, for one, he knows how to protect his money. He won't invest his money in a fool. A good steward isn't wealthy because he's stupid; he's wealthy because he's a good steward. He's good at investing his money.

We need to see money as a means of exchange for souls, and we need to see all the rest of it as dessert. The main course is Kingdom business!

Many will say, "Yes, but I don't have a lot of money right now. How can I be a money missionary?" Remember, I said that to receive the call to be a money missionary, you yield your money to God to use as He sees fit to advance the Kingdom. So it's not a matter of how much you have; it's how you *yield* it that counts! How much are you yielded to His will? Your yielding to His will and His way will change the amount you have.

Right now, you may be so broke that your head cannot handle this discussion! But let these words sink deep into your spirit man. When they take hold and you get the revelation of what I'm saying, it will make you a new person! Your household is going to change. Your bank account is going to change. And it all will happen by the power of God, not by the power of this world system or by your own power.

Your Money Is Soul Money!

Perhaps you have been looking for an answer to your financial dilemmas, saying, "Why, Lord, is it not working out for me? I'm doing all I can." The revelation which you have desired from God has come to answer your cry this day. Don't ask another question—what I'm sharing with you is your answer: *Use your money in exchange for souls!*

Now, when God speaks to you as a money missionary, be careful and diligent to obey Him. Be eager about
it. Be happy! Don't let God have to call you on the
carpet, so to speak, for your disobedience. When you
disobey God, the consequences are twofold: You hinder
the work God wants you to bless, and you hinder yourself.

Let's look again at Luke 16:2: **And he called him, and
said unto him, How is it that I hear this of thee? give
an account of thy stewardship; for thou mayest be no
longer steward.**

As I said, some people used to be money missionaries, but they stopped. They have to repent and get that
straight before God can continue to increase them as they
know they should be increasing. The Lord is calling them
back into stewardship. They can have a fresh new start
and a new beginning. Second Corinthians 5:17 says,
**Therefore if any man be in Christ, he is a new creature:
old things are passed away; behold, all things are
become new.** All their old ways of trying to handle
finances will pass away. God will give them a new way, a
better way.

When I first learned the secret of giving for a living
instead of working for a living, I told the Lord, "Lord, I

am on call twenty-four hours a day. Whatever You want to do with my money is fine with me. I am willing. I'm tired of the old way of handling money; I'm tired of not having enough. I'm tired of just barely getting by. I'm tired of not being able to give "big" into the Kingdom of God. I'm tired of struggling trying to make money—let the money roll!"

I received my call to be a money missionary for God. When a missionary needs money, I am the missionary to that missionary who needs my money for the mission, for the call, for what the Lord has put in his or her heart to do for Him. God didn't send me to a foreign land, but I'm passing out money to those who are sent! And I expect miracles in my finances every day of my life.

Missionaries need not be broke. If the Body of Christ will get hold of this information, God will release a money explosion. Those who are informed, willing, and obedient will get in on it. They'll constantly be receiving miracles in their money. Others will wonder about them, because they'll have so much.

I tell you, I have the solution for every financial dilemma: money in exchange for souls! We've been wringing our hands, fasting, praying, bawling and squalling about money. But we're going to have to pray about something else now, because our money problems are over!

Can you imagine what it's like to have money "up to your ears"? Can you imagine having money stacked up and needing to find more places to give it because you've got so much? But, then, as you find more places to give your money, God keeps blessing you more, and you still have too much money!

We've tried it our way. There is a better way. We've repented of erroneous stewardship. We are getting our priorities straight.

You are called to be a money missionary. You may have other gifts, talents and callings, but no matter what you are called to do, you are also called to yield your money up to God so that He can use it for souls. The only reason we are left here on this earth is to get souls into the Kingdom and to train and disciple souls.

People are at the heart of money's mission, not stuff like houses, cars, clothes and pleasures. Certainly, God wants us to have things and to enjoy life, but we are left here as ambassadors for Christ, the Anointed One. (2 Cor. 5:20.) And through the anointing that He provides to go along with this revelation, we will find freedom from financial problems and lack.

Holding on to Tight Money

There is a liberty in releasing your money to God. It's bondage to try to hold on tight to money when the Spirit of God is trying to get you to turn loose. Obedience to the revelation brings anointing and freedom. It's between you and the Holy Spirit. Nobody can pollute it. It's precious. When the Holy Spirit talks to your heart, and you respond, "Yes, Lord," it touches the heart of God.

Psalm 68:19 says, **Blessed be the Lord, who daily loadeth us with benefits....** Those benefits are not limited to just money, but they certainly include money. And God has loaded me down with the benefit of money. The reason I can preach so freely about money is that I have plenty of it. I'm not after money; I'm just obeying the Lord, saying what He tells me to say.

Someone once said, "Brother Thompson, I don't understand why God anointed you for this money message so much." He continued, "I went to the Lord with it, and the Lord said, *I have anointed him with the money message like I anointed Oral Roberts with the seedtime and harvest message for his generation."*

The Lord went on the tell the man, in effect, *I have anointed Leroy for his generation because he is a pastor and teacher, and I have enabled him to speak to the spirits of men and open the Word to them in this area. They are going to see it and act on it, and I am going to bless them.*

A minister who operates in the office of a prophet gives out revelation by inspiration of the Spirit, and he or she can dump it out suddenly on people; the people have to be ready and on their toes to grab it. But a pastor knows people's hearts, because he lives with them. He's been in the trenches with them. He knows where they've been, where God has brought them from. He has the ability just to talk plainly to people and get them to understand what he's saying. In other words, he can spend time building a foundation and a framework before laying it on them. And God has called me as a pastor and a teacher to proclaim this revelation of financial prosperity.

No More "Digging Duty"!

Let's continue reading Luke 16:3: **Then the steward said within himself, What shall I do? for my lord taketh away from me the stewardship: I cannot dig; to beg I am ashamed.**

Now, once you come into the family of God, you don't have "digging duty" anymore. I'm not saying you don't have to work, but you don't have to work from sunup to sundown by the sweat of your brow, so to speak, for a few dollars. And as a child of God, you don't have it in you now to beg for money. You're not looking for handouts when you are truly living out of your spirit man. Why? Because you know you should be the one giving the handouts!

Your inner man has such an assurance of being taken care of, he just can't go back to the ditches, to the natural way of living. The natural won't please you anymore. You won't be satisfied living the way unbelievers live, just doing the best they can and doing what they know to do. You have divine resources at your disposal.

You're not on your job, digging and begging. No, you're working with dignity and honor and with a confidence in your spirit and a spring in your step. You know that job is not your source; you're a member of a royal Family, and arrangements have been made by your Elder Brother for you to always have more than enough. All you have to do is follow orders from your Father. As a steward, you have to bring your seed to the soil. You have to give it—plant it—so that "more than enough" can come back to you.

So you don't have time to dig and beg. Jehovah Jireh is your Father. You walk in another realm; you can't go back to the beggarly elements of the world system to try to bring finances in. You are walking in a higher dimension, a different world of finances. It's a world of the divine: Your divine Father entrusts to you divine stewardship. He gives you divine orders for divine production and increase to come into your life.

How can you beg anymore? You can't when you give rise to your spirit and to the Greater One within. You are ashamed to live below the level of plenty, the level which God has already brought you up to. You have to continue in faith and obedience until you're living the reality of where you are now in Christ. You can't go back down to the beggarly elements.

Someone asked, "Well, isn't that pride?" No, it's humility, because you know it's God who called you to live in the divine. You know that it would be a slap in the face of God, so to speak, to act as a beggar, poor-mouthing your heavenly Father and talking as if He did not do what He did for you.

You see, all pride is not wrong. You should be proud to be a child of the King. You should be proud that God raised you up to sit in heavenly places in Christ Jesus. (Eph. 2:6.) There should be a certain pride in you so that you can't think like you used to think, do what you used to do or live like you used to live. You are in another Family now.

There might be some help you've been receiving that you can't receive anymore because you've moved; you are on another level now. You are trying to bring others up to where you are; therefore, you can't beg. You are ashamed to go that way because you know that you know that God said He would supply your needs. (Phil. 4:19.) You know Psalm 23:1: **The Lord is my shepherd; I shall not want.** You know that He will not withhold any good thing from them that walk uprightly. (Ps. 84:11.). You can't go back. You're going forward; you're on assignment now. You're a King's child, and you know the King will always pay for the assignments He gives.

If bills are piling up and have you digging, begging and borrowing, then you need to put all those bills in a paper sack, set them in the middle of the floor and just laugh out loud at them. Say, "You had me for a while, but I'm free at last, and you will never have me again. I'm free, free, free!"

Money to pay your bills is not the problem. It's not just money you need—it's stewardship. It's willingness, obedience, faith and anointing. When you believe God and release your money to Him in faith with a willing and obedient heart, the anointing, or power, that you need will be there to cause more money to come to you.

So don't go after money, because money is not the problem. Yieldedness might be the problem. You may be working more than one job or working overtime and not spending time with your family, just trying to bring a little extra money in. You may have your nose to the grindstone, so to speak. But look up! It's not that little bit of money that you need. It's the power of God through your obedience and yieldedness. Money can come in by the droves, not just here and there. But you need to stop digging—working in your own strength and might—and start obeying and believing.

Money in itself is not wrong. The Bible says it's the love of money that is the root of all evil. (1 Tim. 6:10.) But people spend a lot of money to go to college to get money. But there are Ph.D.'s who are more broke than people who don't have an education. I'm not against education. I believe we should be educated. But education is not the answer. Getting an education just to get money is digging. Money won't always follow a college education, but it will always follow obedience and the anointing.

Make a Life Resolution

Let's continue our study of the steward in Luke 16.

Then the steward said within himself, What shall I do? for my lord taketh away from me the stewardship: I cannot dig; to beg I am ashamed.

I am resolved what to do that, when I am put out of the stewardship, they may receive me into their houses.

So he called every one of his lord's debtors unto him, and said unto the first, How much owest thou unto my lord?

And he said, An hundred measure of oil. And he said unto him, Take thy bill, and sit down quickly, and write fifty.

Luke 16:3-6

Look at the phrase in verse 4: **I am resolved what to do…**

The steward's situation is detailed in verses 2 and 3. He had to give an account of his stewardship, and he was fired. Then he asked himself the question, "What am I going to do now? I can't dig, and I'm too ashamed to beg." How many times have we asked ourselves, "I have all these bills—so many that it's all I can see. There are things I need and want, but I can't have them. What am I going to do?"

Well, you can do what this steward did. Verse 4 says he made up his mind about something, and that's what you're going to have to do too.

Evaluate, Repent and Adjust

We are making a life resolution. We have discovered the problem: poor stewardship. That's the first part of the process to evaluate. Then we must resolve to do something about it: repent. Then after we repent, we must also resolve to make an adjustment so that we don't fall back into erroneous stewardship. We must resolve to remain sensitive to God's leading and to be willing and obedient to His instruction.

Tithing: The Prerequisite for Stewardship

Someone said, "Well, I am obedient. After all, I do tithe." Certainly, tithing is correct. You can't be obedient without tithing, because tithing is the will of God. Malachi 3:10 says, **Bring ye all the tithes into the storehouse...** Tithing is elementary, because you can't even begin giving until you're a tither first. The tithe, the tenth, is not a gift; it's something you owe.

Some people tithe and think they are just moving right along on the road of stewardship. But they aren't even on the road yet. They aren't stewards until they start giving, and giving begins beyond the tithe. The tithe is only the foundation; it's not the building itself.

I've talked about being resolved to be a money missionary. When you are resolved to see results in your finances God's way, you are resolved first and foremost to be obedient to Him and His Word. In other words, the thing you are resolved to do is not to get another job, but to make sure you are maintaining your stewardship. When you are resolved and dedicated to obey God, you won't let anyone or anything get in the way of your stewardship.

Stewardship is simple. As a money missionary, as a steward of God's money, your assignment is to pass out that money on the behalf of God. And the more money you pass out, the more He's going to give you to pass out!

I have proven this in my own life and ministry. This is not just something I found and began preaching. I have been practicing this for years, and I am a rich man today because of my stewardship. Some people have the mentality that they can't be rich because of the color of their skin or their family history or what side of the tracks they live on. But none of those things matter. What matters is stewardship.

Covenant Versus Color

For example, I'm not a black man as much as I'm a covenant man! In other words, I'm not paying attention so much to the color of my skin as I am to the fact that I am in Christ, and I am in covenant with God.

People have actually said, "Well, I could believe that prosperity message if I weren't such-and-such color." That is wrong thinking. That's why, years ago, I stopped letting wrong thinking hold me back. Nobody can stop me. Nobody can hold me back from prospering, because I have my hand in the Master's hand! I have the Holy Ghost with me and in me. I am working out my salvation by faith as I learn more and more about the Word of God. (Phil. 2:12.) I'm exploring, discovering, appropriating and living out my covenant, and I can't be stopped!

No matter what race you are, you're not really black, white or any other color. The Word of God says, **There is neither Jew nor Greek, there is neither bond nor free, there is neither male nor female: for ye are all one in Christ Jesus** (Gal. 3:28). In other words, you can't be a good steward if you're thinking black, white and all that other stuff. Also, if you're going to be a good steward, all feelings of superiority and inferiority have to leave you.

Covenant men and women don't see all of that; they just see covenant.

Your Money Pays the Way for the Gospel To Be Preached

Let's continue reading about the steward in Luke 16.

I am resolved what to do, that, when I am put out of the stewardship, they may receive me into their houses.

So HE CALLED EVERY ONE OF HIS LORD'S DEBTORS UNTO HIM, and said unto the first, How much owest thou unto my lord?

And he said, An hundred measures of oil. And he said unto him, Take thy bill, and sit down quickly, and write fifty.

Luke 16:4-6

Notice verse 5: **He called every one of his lord's debtors unto him....** Your money is to be used to call all of the Lord's debtors. There are sinners who are in debt, so to speak, to the Lord, and your money was designed to call them. Your money pays the way for sinners to hear the Gospel and receive Jesus. God wants to use your money to call sinners to the Kingdom of God!

The message of the Gospel is to tell debtors that their debt has been canceled, that through the blood of Jesus Christ, they need no longer be under Satan's dominion. They have been purchased, bought with a price, and that price was the blood of Jesus. Through that Blood, they have been delivered from the power of darkness.

That is what money is for—to pave the way for sinners to hear that their debt of sin has been canceled.

I tell you, when you get hold of this revelation, you will never think the same way about money again. You will stop being overly concerned about your house or your car. You'll just give, and the things you need and want will just show up.

When you get hold of faith and of having a right attitude, or motive, about money, it will be easy to have plenty of it. No man can serve two masters. (Matt. 6:24; Luke 16:13.) Yield to the real Master, and you will master money. Your financial problems will be a thing of the past.

Your giving can change the whole world. It can change the world from the standpoint of having the Gospel preached to the ends of the earth. But it can also change your world as you switch financial systems from the natural to the supernatural, from your way of doing things to God's way of doing things.

Giving can bring such joy to your heart, because you know your prosperity is not coming by the job or by the struggle, but by the Spirit of the living God. It's not even who you know—unless who you know is the covenant-making and covenant-keeping God! With Him, you can get in your prayer closet, get your orders and come out distributing where God tells you to distribute.

You don't have to be concerned about bills anymore. You can look at them and laugh, because you know your help is on the way, and you are boldly declaring it. You know that as you evaluate and then repent and adjust if need be where your stewardship is concerned, your money worries will be over. You won't think about money anymore, except about where to give it. Your emphasis will be on winning men and women into the Kingdom.

You don't have to dig and beg anymore. And you don't have to be kicked around on the job. You are a covenant man or woman, a steward, and every time a tough situation comes up, the wisdom of God will tell you how to handle it. No more natural living for you; you enter into your stewardship confident. You are a steward of God, a representative of Heaven and an ambassador for Christ. You are sent by another Agency that operates in another realm and on another level.

As a money missionary, "Headquarters"—Heaven— will take your case and make supernatural arrangements on your behalf. He'll drop your name somewhere, and provision will be made for you. All you have to do is be willing and obedient and led by the Holy Spirit. He'll make sure you're at the right place at the right time.

You are tracking money for your mission, but soon money will be tracking you! God wants you to stop being average or ordinary. He wants you to live an extra-ordinary life. He wants you to make your money available to Him. He wants houses and cars to show up with your name on them! He wants to work the miraculous in your life.

Say this out loud: "From this day forward, all the money I have and all the money I receive, I will use in exchange for souls. I receive my call as a money missionary to build the Kingdom of God."

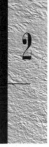

Any revelation from the Word of God needs to be constructed, or built, in your spirit in such a way that it cannot be uprooted or torn down. The deeper the Word sinks into your heart by continual study and meditation, the better able you are to latch on to it and not turn it loose.

In other words, you could get hold of a truth from the Word and then lose it over a period of time through neglect or a lack of understanding. You might lose your initial enthusiasm before fully tapping in to that revelation. You may receive some benefit from that truth, but after awhile, you could begin coasting with the Word you received and lose out on the full benefit.

I believe that is why the Lord told me concerning the message "money with a mission," *Do not reveal this message moderately.*

Remain in Remembrance and Remain Established

When the Lord said that to me, I was reminded of something Peter said in his second epistle.

> **Wherefore I will not be negligent to put you always in REMEMBRANCE of these things, though ye know them, and be ESTABLISHED in the present truth.**
>
> **Yea, I think it meet, as long as I am in this tabernacle, to stir you up by putting you in REMEMBRANCE.**
>
> 2 Peter 1:12,13

Peter was saying that although they had already heard the truth, he was repeating it to them to stir them up. He wasn't going to just preach the message moderately and let it fall by the wayside.

According to this passage, the people must have previously heard the truth, because Peter said he was putting them in *remembrance* (you can't be put in remembrance of something you have never even heard before). Verse 12 says, **...put you always in remembrance of these things, THOUGH YE KNOW THEM....**

I believe that's why God was telling me not to preach this message moderately. If I don't continue putting people in remembrance, they will let it slip. But if I continue to stir you up with this truth, verse 12 says you will be *established* in it.

God once told me that there was a multiplicity of anointing that He has placed on the Body of Christ for prosperity, but it can't affect them the way He wants it to unless somebody continually preaches and teaches the revelation.

I believe that the revelation of "money with a mission" will put you in remembrance, establish you in the truth of divine prosperity, and take you further besides. As I said in the last chapter, money is not just for buying houses, cars and clothes and putting in your accounts and in your pocket for you, you, you! No, your money—the money God gives you—has a specific assignment, a mission.

When you talk about money, some people think about a whole lot of other things besides money's assignment. They have forgotten the Lord. But we need to understand that God's vision for the world has to be backed somehow, and that includes its being backed financially. Well, who is supposed to financially back

God's vision, the preaching of the Gospel and the harvesting of souls? *Wealthy Christians!*

Someone said, "Well, that leaves me out. I'm a Christian, but I'm not wealthy." But God is trying to tell you how to get wealthy!

Millionaire Status

Did you know that every Christian has millionaire status on the inside of him or her? Now, does that mean that every Christian will become a millionaire? No, but it is possible.

God knows, we know, and even the devil and demons know that God has provided through the Lord Jesus Christ the possibility of everyone being saved. But we know that everyone will not be saved. Not everyone will accept the free gift of salvation by accepting Jesus Christ as Savior and Lord.

God has also provided through Christ the possibility of everyone being healed. But we know that everyone who needs healing will not be healed; not everyone will receive healing.

Similarly, God has provided through Christ the possibility of everyone being rich. I know that sounds shocking, but it is the truth. Yet not everyone will be rich, because some will not accept it. Some will not accept the conditions for prosperity even though they have millionaire status on the inside of them.

What are the conditions for prosperity? Accepting the call to be a money missionary and to use money first for its assignment instead of hoarding it for just you and your family and some of your friends. You have millionaire status on the inside of you, but it is millionaire status for the Kingdom with a Kingdom purpose. When the mission is understood more than anything else and acted upon, the millionaire status is released.

You can actually get to the place in life where you can say in faith, meaning it with all your heart, "I will never be broke another day in my life." Those words spoken with power will bring power to cause it to be so in your life. God told me to tell that to His people. He wants you to say it because it is anointed. So say out loud, "I'll never be broke another day in my life!"

You can get to a place where you become a "money magnet." In other words, money will be attracted to you. But it is money with an assignment. You just become the channel whereby that money can flow and fulfill its assignment.

As I said, all believers, no matter what their last name, the color of their skin, or their background, has millionaire status inside them. Prosperity is the will of God for you! The Holy Ghost, who knows where all the money is, will reveal prosperity to you personally if you will answer the call.

Again, don't misunderstand me and say, "Brother Thompson said that every believer is going to be a millionaire." No, I didn't say every believer is going to be a millionaire. But it is possible. I am a living testimony of that fact.

Many years ago, it didn't look possible for me, but I am a millionaire today because I accepted the call to be a money missionary. My money, the money God gives me, has a mission, an assignment. I gave (I still give) when and where God told me to give, and I am a blessed man today as a result.

When you see your money as money with a mission, God will bless you with extras. He will say, *Since you did that for Me, I'm going to do this for you.*

Remember the Lord

You remember I said that where the Word of God is concerned, there is a connection between *remembering* and *being established.* Let's look at a familiar verse to further illustrate that fact.

> **But thou shalt REMEMBER the Lord thy God: for it is he that giveth thee power to get wealth, that he may ESTABLISH his covenant which he sware unto thy fathers, as it is this day.**
>
> **Deuteronomy 8:18**

This verse is written in a different context than 2 Peter 1:12-13, but the truth is still the same. Deuteronomy 8:18 says that God will establish His covenant (a covenant of prosperity) when you do something. When you do what? When you *remember the Lord!*

Why are you to remember the Lord? This verse tells you why: **...for it is he that giveth thee power to get wealth... !**

Let's go back and read the surrounding verses in Deuteronomy 8.

And thou shalt REMEMBER all the way which the Lord thy God led thee these forty years in the wilderness, to humble thee, and to prove thee, to know what was in thine heart, whether thou wouldest keep his commandments, or no.

Therefore thou shalt KEEP the commandments of the Lord thy God, to walk in his ways, and to fear him.

For the Lord thy God bringeth thee into a good land, a land of brooks of water, of fountains and depths that spring out of valleys and hills; a land of wheat, and barley, and vines, and fig trees, and pomegranates; a land of oil olive, and honey; a land wherein thou shalt eat bread without scarceness, thou shalt not lack any thing in it; a land whose stones are iron, and out of whose hills thou mayest dig brass.

When thou hast eaten and art full, then thou shalt bless the Lord thy God for the good land which he hath given thee.

Beware that thou FORGET NOT the Lord thy God, in not keeping his commandments, and his judgments, and his statutes, which I command thee this day: lest when thou hast eaten and art full, and hast built goodly houses, and dwelt therein; and when thy herds and thy flocks multiply, and thy silver and thy gold is multiplied, and all that thou hast is multiplied; then thine heart be lifted up, and thou forget the Lord thy God, which brought thee forth out of the land of Egypt, from the house of bondage.

And thou say in thine heart, My power and the might of mine hand hath gotten me this wealth.

Deuteronomy 8:2,6-14,17

Now let's read verse 18 again:

But thou shalt REMEMBER THE LORD THY GOD: for it is he that giveth thee power to get wealth, that he may establish his covenant which he sware unto thy fathers, as it is this day.

This passage makes a definite connection between remembering the Lord and being blessed as a result.

Remembering—the Key to Obedience and Blessing

God can't establish His covenant in the life of a believer who is not remembering Him and His Word. We know that throughout the Word, God stresses obedience as a requirement for receiving His blessing. Well, if you're not remembering, you're not going to obey. You can't obey what you're not _remembering_.

So remembering the Lord is how we get in a position to obey. And obeying is how we get in a position to receive.

If ye be willing and obedient, ye shall eat the good of the land.

Isaiah 1:19

To eat the good of the land, you have to be obedient to the Lord and His Word, and you have to be willing. What does that mean in the context of Deuteronomy 8? It means you have to be willing and obedient to put God's business first before your own. In other words, you have to put first His vision of preaching the Gospel and harvesting souls around the world. Then you will be blessed; you will eat the good of the land, the best the land has to offer.

I'm eating the good of the land today, because I have God's business as my first priority. I live in the best; I drive the best, and I wear the best because I give God my best. My money's first mission is not to buy houses, cars and clothes. No, my money's mission is to do what the Lord wants to do with it.

You see, when God knows that you are remembering Him and putting Him first, He starts being free with you. In other words, the blessings start flowing.

Remember the Lord With Your Money

It is not enough just to remember the Lord with lip service, saying, "Oh, Lord, I remember You." When you are truly remembering the Lord and His Word, you are doing something. You are obeying what He tells you to do. And you cannot obey the whole counsel of God's Word without tithing, giving offerings and dedicating yourself and your money to God's work, to put Him first and to do with your money what He wants you to do.

Going back to Deuteronomy 8:18, let me explain in detail what it means to remember the Lord with your money. Did you know that your money can be a memorial to the Lord?

What is a memorial? It is a remembrance; a recollection; something intended to preserve in memory a person or event; a commemoration.

When you see your money as money with a mission and you give it first to the Lord's work, your money becomes a memorial, a token of remembrance, or recollection, of what the Lord has done for you and of the fact that He, not the world, is your source. Your money is used to preserve in memory the Lord Jesus Christ and the act of redemption that He consummated on your behalf. It preserves in memory and commemorates the fact that you are redeemed from the curse of the Law, including the curse of poverty.

Well, Deuteronomy 8 tells us to remember the Lord, and it is especially talking about remembering Him in connection with your material blessings. We are to remember Him as our source. We are to remember where He brought us from. We are to remember we couldn't get to where we are without Him. Even if we are behind, if we are better off than we were before, it is He who bettered us. And we need to remember that. With all of that in remembrance, it should be easy to remember the Lord with your money and to put Him first.

When the Lord knows that you have Him in full remembrance, He knows that He can trust you. God doesn't just bless you with millions overnight. No, He gives you smaller blessings first to see how you are going to act. When you get money and the first thing that comes to your mind is the Lord and His work, you know you are getting there.

If you don't have a revelation of the mission, you can't have the money. But God does want you to have money, and He wants to give it to you. Deuteronomy 8:18 says, ...**for it is he that giveth thee power to get wealth, that he may establish his covenant which he sware unto thy fathers, as it is this day.**

God gives the power to get wealth, and He does it to establish His covenant. How do we make the covenant connection? By doing the first part of that verse: ...**remember the Lord thy God....**

This is where the Church has been robbed. The Church at large has not had the revelation of the mission. They can't get the money they need, because they haven't been remembering the Lord. But I believe God's people are getting the revelation like never before and are going to operate on a different level in their finances from now on.

To remember the Lord with your money is to remember His mission with your money. There are billions of people who haven't heard the Gospel yet. Certainly, we are to be a light and a witness in our own world in our neighborhoods and communities but God has called many to go forth into the nations of the world with the Gospel message of salvation through Jesus Christ. It takes finances to do that.

When you remember the Lord's mission with your money, you release God's ability to establish His covenant with you. His ability is released in your finances, and you are on your way to another level financially.

Now, you are always going to have some whiners and criers who don't understand why you are so blessed. But you can't stop to answer that or even be bothered with it, because you are too busy about your Father's business; you are too busy remembering and obeying and being blessed!

Let's read another passage of Scripture that talks about remembering.

And when he had given thanks, he brake it, and said, Take, eat: this is my body, which is broken for you: this do in REMEMBRANCE of me. After the same manner also he took the cup, when he had supped, saying, This cup is the new testament in my blood: this do ye, as oft as ye drink it, in REMEMBRANCE of me.

1 Corinthians 11:24,25

Why did Jesus tell us to take Communion in remembrance of Him? So we could rehearse and keep fresh in our minds what He did for us in His death, burial and resurrection. Similarly, our giving to God's work should be a memorial commemorating what God has done and will continue to do for us financially as we obey Him. He purchased salvation in redemption, and He also purchased our prosperity. So there is a connection between Deuteronomy 8:18 and 1 Corinthians 11:25, between the covenant and Communion.

In the Old Testament, the curse for breaking God's Law was threefold. It included poverty, sickness and disease, and spiritual death. But the Bible says, **Christ hath redeemed us from the curse of the law, being made a curse for us: for it is written, Cursed is every one that hangeth on a tree** (Gal. 3:13).

Christ redeemed us from poverty and lack, and we
need to remember that fact. We need to remember the
Lord with our money and allow it to be used as a
memorial to Him for His great goodness to us and to
the whole world.

Our money can be a memorial to the Lord as a token
of our remembrance of Him and what He has done for
us. But did you know that when we give our money
toward God's mission, it creates a memorial in the mind
of God about us? It creates a memorial of our faithfulness and trustworthiness. And once that memorial is
created in God's mind, He never forgets.

Let's look at a New Testament example of someone
who created a memorial for herself.

> **There came unto him a woman having an
> alabaster box of very precious ointment, and
> poured it on his [Jesus'] head, as he sat at meat.**
>
> **But when his disciples saw it, they had indig-
> nation, saying, To what purpose is this waste?**
>
> **For this ointment might have been sold for
> much, and given to the poor.**

When Jesus understood it, he said unto them, Why trouble ye the woman? for she hath wrought a good work upon me.

For ye have the poor always with you; but me ye have not always.

For in that she hath poured this ointment on my body, she did it for my burial.

Verily I say unto you, Wheresoever this gospel shall be preached in the whole world, there shall also this, that this woman hath done, be told for a memorial of her.

Matthew 26:7-13

Money with a mission is money that creates a memorial in the mind of God of your faithfulness. Because this woman gave her best—her expensive perfume—to Jesus, she received the stamp of approval that she was in financial covenant with Almighty God. She was a marked woman! I believe that when Jesus said that her act of faithfulness would be a memorial to her, millionaire status—the supernatural favor of God for finances—came upon that woman's life. A financial anointing was released upon her, and I believe money began to hunt her down after that.

I am living in that financial anointing. Money hunts me down wherever I go. I don't go looking for it; it looks for me. When you get a financial anointing, and you get under the favor of God, money doesn't matter anymore. Money is just looking for you; it wants to come to you. Money wants to be with you because you have good spiritual sense! Money knows that you are going to do the right thing with it. It knows that you are going to remember the Lord.

As we honor God with our money because He has been so good to us (we know it was He who gave us that money to start with), God will honor us. As we remember Him with our money, we set up a memorial in our own lives in the mind of God, and He will favor us in return. Then as our money is used to propagate the Gospel, our money sets up a memorial before others of God's goodness and of His saving power so that His mission can be accomplished in the earth.

3

Agree with God, and be at peace;
thereby good will come to you.
—JOB 22:21, RSV

Agreeing with God and being submitted to Him is
agreeing and submitting to His Word—both His
holy written Word and His spoken word, the word He
may speak to you. We can't be in full submission to the
Father and His Word without being fully submitted in
our finances too.

Did you know that your money can agree with God?
Your money can also disagree with God. The choice is
yours. Are you giving in submission to Him, releasing
your finances to His will, or are you holding on tight in
opposition and irreverence to Him? Great peace and
great good will come to you when you are in full agreement and submission to God in every area of your life,
including the financial area.

"Circumcised" Money Is Blessed Money!

Now, I've said this many times before, but I cannot talk about giving offerings without mentioning the tithe, the ten percent: *Your tithe is not an offering; it's something you owe. Therefore, you are not even giving until you are tithing first.* Your offerings are what you give over and beyond the tithe. Your paying that ten percent "circumcises" your money, so to speak. If you are not tithing, you are walking around with uncircumcised money, which God cannot bless.

In other words, that ten percent puts your money under the anointing. When you tithe, you put the rest of your money—the ninety percent—under the blessing. It is "circumcised." That money cannot fall down and fail to do the job because it is in agreement with God and with the covenant.

> **Honour the Lord with thy substance, and with the firstfruits of all thine increase:so shall thy barns be filled with plenty, and thy presses shall burst out with new wane.**
>
> **Proverbs 3:9,10**

**Bring ye all the tithes into the storehouse,
that there may be meat in mine house, and
prove me now herewith, saith the Lord of hosts,
if I will not open you the windows of heaven,
and pour you out a blessing, that there shall not
be room enough to receive it.**

Malachi 3:10

Many people are not experiencing the blessings promised in these verses because they are not meeting the requirements. They are getting nowhere in their finances because they are over-concerned about their own mission and under-concerned about God's mission. It's as if these people are on a treadmill in their finances; they are moving and making an effort to prosper, but they are getting nowhere.

To put God's mission first—to be a money missionary—you have to have what I call a *ministry* of giving. (God doesn't call just a few to this ministry—this is one ministry we all should have.)

In other words, you are giving consistently, not just here and there. You don't need a lot of money for that. We just read Proverbs 3:9, **Honour the Lord with THY substance, and with the firstfruits of all THINE increase.** This verse doesn't say to honor the Lord with "thy large substance" or "thine big increase." No, it just says to honor the Lord with your own substance and increase, whatever it may be. Now notice the next verse.

So shall thy barns be filled with plenty, and thy presses shall burst out with new wine.

Proverbs 3:10

These two verses reveal cause and effect relationship. In verse 9, the Lord said to honor Him with your substance and with the firstfruits of your increase. The Lord never tells us to do something unless He has some blessing in mind for us. So, first, He said to give. Then He said that as a result of your giving of the firstfruits (tithing), your barns will be filled—that is, you will receive a financial blessing.

Substance, Seed and Supply

In Proverbs 3:9-10, we see in motion a principle I call *substance, seed* and *supply.* In other words, you honor God with your substance; He returns it to you in the form of seed, which you sow again, and He makes sure you are always supplied.

Why does God want you to give so that He can give back to you? *So you can honor Him again so He can honor you again!* You become an asset to the Lord and His Kingdom when you honor Him with your money.

In return, the Lord begins to "side in" with you as a business partner, so to speak. He knows where all favor, promotion and increase are, and He will reveal it to you because He knows what you are going to do with it. He knows that you are going to honor Him with your substance and with the firstfruits of all your increase.

Even in the natural, in the business world, a company which hires someone they believe will be a great asset to them will not pay him a salary allowing him only enough to live in government subsidized housing. No, they want him to have a nice house, wear nice clothes and represent them well. They want his mind clear and sharp. They will not mishandle him; they will reward him. When he leaves his house in the morning, he is undisturbed by worry over finances and ready to benefit that company and do the job they hired him to do.

Similarly, when you get on God's mission, you are going to financially pass up your fellow Christians who are griping and complaining about the prosperity message and being stingy with the money God has given them.

This is no gimmick. God wants you to go forward in your finances, and He wants you to do it supernaturally so that you and others will know it is He who is bringing you forward. If you will hear this message and heed it, you will get more and sweat less.

You see, your education has not done it. We have more educated people in the Body of Christ than you can imagine, but, sadly, many of them are broke! They have no money, or they don't have enough money. They are struggling.

As I said, many are not living out Proverbs 3:9-10. They might be "confessing" that they are, but they're not experiencing the blessings. I'm trying to show you how to move from just *confessing* something to *living* it! I want to tell you that it is possible. My barns are filled with plenty, and that plenty didn't come out of the pockets of my church members. It came and continues to come as a result of my answering the call to be a money missionary and doing what Proverbs 3:9-10 says to do.

I tell you, not everything that makes you feel "goose bumps" is worth listening to. (Goose bumps aren't worth much at all. Just go to a nice restaurant after feeling goose bumps in the service at church one Sunday. When the check comes, just write "goose bumps" on it and see how far it gets you!)

But what I'm telling you is real. You might get angry, because you don't want the Lord interfering with your money. Or you might hear the message and never do anything about it. But if you hear and heed in faith, your "broke" days are going to be over.

> **I love them that love me; and those that seek me early shall find me; riches and honour are with me; yea, DURABLE riches and righteousness.**
>
> **Proverbs 8:17,18**

Look at that phrase, **durable riches and righteousness.** Remember, at the end of the first chapter, I asked you to confess out loud, "I'll never be broke another day in my life." You can make that confession because of what God says in these verses in Proverbs. When you seek God and His wisdom first, putting His Word first and foremost in your life in your words and actions, riches and honor will come to you—**yea, DURABLE riches and righteousness.**

Durable means long-lasting. That's why I can say I'll never be broke another day in my life. My riches are long-lasting; I have durable riches now. They are not riches I received as the result of my own strength. God and I are partners, and He and I are never going to be broke! It doesn't matter what comes up—depression, recession, oppression or any kind of "-ession"—I'll never be broke another day in my life! I'm in partnership with the supernatural Almighty God, and He's going to take care of me. I'm not leaving Him, and He will never leave me.

Not Enough Just To Know It

I'm trying to get you to see what is available to you, but, really, it's not enough just to know it's available. You have to do some things to get there, and I believe you are going to get there.

Let's continue reading in Proverbs 8.

My fruit is better than gold, yea, than fine gold; and my revenue than choice silver.

I lead in the way of righteousness, in the midst of the patina of judgment: that I may

cause those that love me to inherit substance; and I will fill their treasures.

Proverbs 8:19-21

Look at verse 21: **That I may** CAUSE **those that love me to inherit substance....** That means God will make it happen for you!

Now, what kind of substance is God talking about? It's a particular kind of substance, a substance that's connected with His mission. Remember, I talked about substance, seed and supply. I said that God gives the seed and the supply when you honor Him with your substance, but, really, He gives the substance too!

And it came to pass afterward, that he [Jesus] went throughout every city and village, preaching and shewing the glad tidings of the kingdom of God: and the twelve were with him, and certain women, which had been healed of evil spirits and infirmities, Mary called Magdalene, out of whom went seven devils, and Joanna the wife of Chuza Herod's steward, and Susanna, and many others, which MINISTERED UNTO HIM OF THEIR SUBSTANCE.

Luke 8:1-3

Before I talk about ministering to the Lord with your substance, I want to focus on verse 2 for a minute: **And certain women, which had been healed of evil spirit. and infirmities, Mary called Magdalene, out of whom went seven devils.**

The Word of God says that he (or she) who has been forgiven much loves much. (Luke 7:47.) Mary Magdalene had been forgiven of much and helped much, and she loved much. She loved the Lord, and she loved His work. Some people do not appreciate the magnitude of God's love and mercy because they don't realize how much they really need Him. For example, they'll say, "Well, I've never smoked or drunk. I've never committed adultery. I've always fulfilled my responsibilities in life. I've paid my bills, and I've supported my family." But if they don't know Jesus as Savior, all of that "good living" is in vain; they are still lost and in sin.

He Who Is Forgiven Much, Loves Much— He Who Loves Much, *Gives* Much!

Some people go to church and think they are doing the pastor a favor by being there gracing him with their presence. Then they sit there in the pew with their Bibles closed acting like they're better than everybody else. They don't love and appreciate the Lord or His people. And they certainly don't love and appreciate the minister.

At the other extreme, there are others who have messed up badly in life. They made wrong choices, which landed them in the gutter and the muck and the mire of sin. They knew they needed mercy and grace. They had no good works to stand on or to boast about. So they turned to Jesus for forgiveness. They accepted Him as Savior and Lord, and He forgave them, delivered them and made them brand-new.

Do you know that a person in that category could be more appreciative of God's mercy and grace than a person who has always lived an upstanding life?

I tell you what, I'm really appreciative of the Lord, and you should be too! Whether you have a rough background filled with mistake after mistake, or you've led a sheltered life and never ventured out into a riotous lifestyle, you should appreciate the fact that when mankind needed a Savior, Jesus Christ paid the price for sin and became that Savior.

The Bible says, **For ALL have sinned, and come short of the glory of God** (Rom. 3:23).

I can relate to Paul. He said he was the chiefest of sinners. (1 Tim. 1:15.) I knew that I needed to be forgiven. The Lord saved me, filled me with His Spirit and set my life on a new, solid foundation. **I am not ashamed of the gospel of Christ, for it is the power of God unto salvation to every one that believeth** (Rom. 1:16).

I know I didn't deserve salvation, but none of us deserves it; it is a gift. I just accepted the gift—the riches of His grace—by faith, and I love Him for it.

That's the way it was with Mary Magdalene. Jesus had cast seven devils out of her and had set her free. She loved Him. She appreciated Him. She was very aware of Jesus' mercy in her life, and she loved Him for it.

Luke goes on to talk about other women: **And JOANNA the wife of Chuza Herod's steward, and SUSANNA, and MANY OTHERS...**(v. 3). Notice what it says about them: **...WHICH MINISTERED UNTO HIM [Jesus] OF THEIR SUBSTANCE.**

These women ministered unto Jesus with their substance—with their money. They had a money ministry. They saw their money as money with a mission, an assignment. They wanted to support the Lord and His work so that more people could be delivered, helped and blessed as they had been.

Maybe you can say along with Mary Magdalene and others, "Lord, I appreciate what You've done for me. Because of You, I have peace instead of torment. Because of You, I can sleep at night. Those demons wouldn't let me rest, but You have set me free. I don't need the psychics anymore. They couldn't help me. But You came along and touched me, and I am delivered! No psychic is going to get my money. I'm putting my money into Your business. I don't need the casinos anymore. No casino is going to get my money. I'm putting my money in Your hands. I don't need the drug dealers anymore. No dope peddler is going to get my money. I'm giving my money to You."

But of course you can't have a money ministry if money is not coming to you. Certainly, it's not the amount you give, and you have to start where you are. You have to be faithful with what little you have before God can increase you the way He wants to. But if money isn't coming to you, you can't very well have a money ministry. That's why God gave the revelation "Money cometh." He wanted the Body of Christ to understand that it's His will that we have money. But He wants us to know what that money is for. It's for a purpose, and that purpose is souls.

Money With an Assignment

Money with an assignment has an anointing on it. It will prosper in the assignment designated for that money, and it will prosper and increase the giver. You see, money is just money, but when it gets in the hands of a money missionary, it changes characteristics, so to speak. It becomes anointed.

Some in the Body of Christ go to the mission field, but most of us don't. We are the ones who are supposed to "send" those called to go. We are supposed to have the same attitude those women had in Luke 8. We are supposed to appreciate what the Lord has done for us and desire that others get in on what we have. Mary Magdalene no doubt said, "Jesus cast seven demons out of me. He delivered me, and I am free indeed. I want somebody else to experience this freedom I have. I'm going to support the Lord with my substance."

That's what it means to have a money ministry and to be a money missionary. It's not about material things.

God will give you anything that you even think about if you stick with the mission instead of trying to get things for yourself. Some people struggle and scheme to buy the kind of car they want, and then that car becomes their glory. Their identity is wrapped up in that car.

Our glory should be in the Lord and what He is doing in the earth. Our glory should lie in the fact that we know He will supply material blessings because we are taking care of His business first.

God is not holding anything back from you. And the *devil* isn't holding anything back from you—he can't hold things back that belong to you. Only you can hold yourself back by forgetting money's purpose and failing to agree with God and His Word with your money.

God Has More in Store for You!

Some haven't been blessed the way God wants to bless them because they've been holding on too tightly to money. Determine in your heart to turn your money loose when God says to turn it loose. Whatever He says to you, do it, no matter how crazy it seems. When He tells you to give, just know that He has something more in store for you. He won't pass you by, but you have to learn to trust Him and to be in agreement with Him concerning money. When He tells you to do something with your money, you can't decide not to do it and expect to be blessed.

As I said, agreeing with God is agreeing with His Word. I've said this many times: You could use Bible faith and still be broke because you are not agreeing with other parts of the Word, which say, for example, to give and it shall be given unto you. (Luke 6:38.)

On the other hand, you could give and be broke because you don't know how to agree with God concerning His will for your prosperity, or you don't know how to use your faith according to the Word. In other words, you either aren't convinced that God wants to prosper you, or you don't know how to receive divine prosperity by faith. You don't know how to get your heart and your mouth in agreement with the covenant of prosperity that God has provided.

For example, Mark ll:23 says, **For verily I say unto you, That whosoever shall say unto this mountain, Be thou removed, and be thou cast into the sea; and shall not doubt in his heart, but shall believe that those things which he saith shall come to pass; he shall have**

whatsoever he saith. Yet instead of saying what they want to come to pass, many talk about what they don't have. Instead of saying, "Money cometh," they'll say, "Money goeth," or "I never have enough. Money is short." And they are having what they're saying! They're not agreeing with God.

Learn to put your mind in agreement with God and His Word. The Bible says, **Can two walk together, except they be agreed?** (Amos 3:3). When your money agrees with God's mission, and your heart and mouth agree with God's covenant, God becomes your business partner. You're saying to Him, "Lord, what I have is Yours," and He's saying to you, "What *I* have is *yours.*"

We've never connected money with the mission, and the devil has gotten away with his lies, telling Christians, *Be holy: Stay away from money. Money is evil.*

Every time someone begins to move out into financial increase, the devil rises up to accuse that person, saying, *You can't have money and please God.* But those statements don't agree with God.

Some people don't want to hear about money in connection with the Lord. They just want to hear about grace. But did you know that grace is involved in money too?

Therefore, as ye abound in every thing, in faith, and utterance, and knowledge, and in all diligence, and in your love to us, SEE THAT YE ABOUND IN THIS GRACE ALSO.

For ye know the GRACE **of our Lord Jesus Christ, that, though he was rich, yet for your sakes he became poor, that ye through his poverty might be rich** [rich with a mission!].

2 Corinthians 8:7,9

Why do you suppose God put us in a position to be rich through Jesus' poverty? He wants us to be rich, but He wants us to be rich with a mission—rich to finish what Jesus started when He was on the earth. John 3:16 says, **For God so loved the world, that he gave his only begotten Son, that whosoever believeth in him should not perish, but have everlasting life.** That is why God wants you to be rich—so the world can have the Gospel preached unto them so that they might hear the Word, believe it, call on the name of the Lord and be saved. (Rom. 10:13,14.)

But the world can't have the Gospel unless God has your money. God can't give you money and make you rich until you are willing to give it up. But if you are always holding on tight and clamoring for more money,

money will end up hurting you. That's why you have to understand the mission—that the Gospel go forth. The Word says that the Macedonian church gave out of their need because they knew the system had to go on. They gave that others could hear the Gospel. **How that in a great trial of affliction the abundance of their (the Macedonians) joy and their deep poverty abounded unto the riches of their liberality** (2 Cor. 8:2.)

You see, we have to have the mind of Christ (1 Cor. 2:16) when we are forming opinions about God and money. We have to agree with God and get our money-hooked up with Him in a divine connection.

A lot of the prayers and confessions we've been making for money could be better used to get people into the Kingdom of God. Many are working two jobs and don't have time to tell anyone about Jesus or to care about missions and the preaching of the Gospel around the world. They are too busy trying to put a piece of wholesome bread on the table.

We weren't created to work two and three jobs, going from sunup to sundown just trying to make it through financially. How can a parent work two and three jobs and have a happy, healthy, successful family unit that glorifies God?

There is a way to prosper God's way, but we have to stop waiting for things to happen by accident; we have to make them happen on purpose. Just saying, "I love Jesus," won't cut it. We have to agree with God with our money and with our mouths!

As you and your money agree with God—as you make your money available to God in faith—expect to get out of debt. Expect to increase and prosper. Expect good to come to you as you hook up with God and His mission with your money. Your money can agree with God, and, as it does, it can't help but grow, increase, multiply and bless your life and the lives of others.

God wants you to have money, and there is a reason why He wants you to have it. God has a financial covenant for His people, but they have to get past Satan's lies, human reasoning, wrong teaching and the traditions of men in order to get in on it. Religious teaching has said that Christians shouldn't have money; they should be broke. Christians have been held back thinking about that rich young ruler (Mark 10:17-31), the rich farmer (Luke 12:16-21), and the rich man and Lazarus (Luke 16:19-31).

These Christians remembered that Jesus said that it was easier for a camel to go through the eye of a needle than for a rich man to enter the Kingdom of Heaven (Matt. 19:24; Mark 10:25; Luke 18:25), and they've been afraid of riches. (It's true that it is easier for a camel to get down and inch its way through an eye of a needle— a small gateway used in certain fortified cities years ago—than it is for a man who is trusting in uncertain riches to turn his trust over to God. That's what this verse is talking about.)

Many dedicated, well-meaning Christians believe preachers who misquote 1 Timothy 6:10, saying, "Money is the root of all evil," without even looking up the verse. They have maintained a position of avoiding the subject of prosperity, and some have even taken vows of poverty. They've wanted to do the right thing, but they've been misled. They've said, "I don't want to go any further. I'm satisfied where I am. The Lord will take care of me." But they haven't understood the reason God wants them to have money.

There is Kingdom business to be taken care of, and it is the Church's responsibility to take care of it. It's a Christian mission, and it's going to take Christians' money to carry it out. So Christians need to find out how to tap in to God's financial covenant and become recipients of what He wants them to have. That covenant made it possible for every believer to carry an anointing to be prosperous with a mission.

As I said, God has a financial covenant for His people. But the world has a covenant too. You see, anything that God does, Satan will try to duplicate or counterfeit. And he is the god of this world system. (2 Cor. 4:4.) But the world's covenant is designed to break you and make you a driven, nervous wreck, clamoring for more money. And the world is in on the lie that Christians should be satisfied being broke. The world has had Christians thinking that sinners should be spending millions on bars, dance-halls, and high-rise casinos while Christians should barely be getting by in their worn-down church buildings barely able to pay the light bill.

In order to tap in to God's financial covenant, Christians have to be willing to be taught scripturally and to change their minds if their thinking doesn't line up with the truth of God's Word. They have to be willing to hear and not be "traditionally deaf" to what the Spirit of God is saying. And, ultimately, they are going to have to position themselves beyond just their job in obtaining finances. (That job is not the only way to receive money. You have to put yourself in a position where God can bless you multiplied times beyond what any job can pay you.)

The Mission-Money Connection

There is a definite connection between God's mission and your money. Often, how much money a person has is a result of how he has connected what money he had, whether it was a little or a lot, with God's mission and His work.

> **Verily, verily, I say unto you, He that believeth on me, the WORKS that I do shall he do also; and greater works than these shall he do; because I go unto my Father.**
>
> **John 14:12**

This verse is talking to Christians. Jesus was talking to those who *believed* in Him. He told us that we are going to do the works that He did, and even greater works, because He was going to His Father. What are the greater works the Church is supposed to be doing? They can't be a greater quality of works, because we know that Jesus had the Spirit without measure. (John 3:34.) We have the Spirit of God by measure, or in a measure. So these "greater works" have to be dealing with quantity. We as the entire Body of Christ together have to do a greater quantity of works, because we have more territory—the world—to cover than Jesus did when He was on the earth.

> **Go ye into all the world, and preach the Gospel to every creature.**

He that believeth and is baptized shall be
saved; but he that believeth not shall be damned.

And these signs shall follow them that
believe; In my name shall they cast out devils;
they shall speak with new tongues; they shall
take up serpents; and if they drink any deadly
thing, it shall not hurt them; they shall lay
hands on the sick, and they shall recover.

Mark 16:15-18

Going into all the world and doing the works of Jesus
is going to take more than prayer. Going into all the
world is going to take more than being spiritually "deep"
and just talking and philosophizing about going. No,
going into all the world is going to take some money—
silver and gold! And the Lord wants you to be a pipeline
He can channel His money through.

The earth is the Lord's, and the fulness
thereof; the world, and they that dwell therein.

Psalm 24:1

For every beast of the forest is mine, and the
cattle upon a thousand hills.

...for the world is mine, and the fulness thereof.

Psalm 50:10,12

The silver is mine, and the gold is mine, saith the Lord of hosts.

Haggai 2:8

All the silver and all the gold and the world and the fulness thereof belong to God. He gave it to the first man, Adam. Adam was a wealthy man. He was in dominion— he was in authority. But then he sold out to Satan through disobedience to God, and Satan became the god of this world.

Jesus gave us authority over all the power of the enemy. (Luke 10:19.) As Christians, we are to rule and reign in life by Him. (Rom. 5:17.) I would like to see Christians come to the point where they are dominating circumstances instead of allowing circumstances to dominate them.

God wants you dominating in every area of your life. You can't just dominate in your prayer life and be successful. You have to dominate in health, and you have to dominate in wealth.

When the Lord dealt with me about money with a mission, He said to me, *Tell the Body of Christ that the mission is more important than the money, but the money is important to the mission.* The money and the mission are a divine combination.

Some people don't want to use the word "divine" in connection with money. They don't see the connection between the mission and money. But if the Gospel is preached and people get saved, that's divine, isn't it? If the Gospel is preached, and a family is brought out of a distressing situation, that's divine. If the Gospel is preached, and the sick are restored and made well, that's divine too.

There is a connection between the mission and money. The mission cannot be accomplished without our giving. I mentioned in a previous chapter that giving is a grace, and we are all called to appropriate this grace. Second Corinthians 8:9 says, **For ye know the grace of our Lord Jesus Christ, that, though he was rich, yet for your sakes he became poor, that ye through his poverty might be rich.**

Our prosperity is a grace. Our being financially able to withstand anything that comes against our families is a grace. Our being able to take care of our families without the help of the world system is a grace. And our being prompt-to-do-it givers, ready at all times to meet the cause, is a grace.

Don't Forfeit Your Grace

If you don't make a covenant with God, you are going to make a covenant with the world. If you don't make a financial covenant with Almighty God, you are going to make a financial covenant with this world system. Sad to say, many Christians have made a covenant with this world system because they don't know what tithes and offerings are really all about. They don't understand the importance and the benefits of obedience to the Word in the area of finances, and they don't understand the law of giving and receiving.

When the preacher mentions money in church, these Christians think he is just trying to put money in his pocket. Many pastors have resorted to begging the people for money to meet the needs of the church, but you shouldn't have to beg for a gift. In other words, if the people really understood what the Bible has to say about giving and receiving, pastors would never have to ask for money.

Reaping Without a Revelation

One of the greatest revelations you can receive is the revelation of God as a Giver. If you really knew Him as a Giver, you would know that He is not playing games with you; He is not teasing you. This revelation is greater than the revelation of reaping, because if you really know God as a Giver, reaping is no problem.

We have held reaping in high priority, and we've been trying to reap without a revelation. As a result, we haven't been able to maintain our reaping. We couldn't reap consistently because the thing that keeps us consistent in our reaping is the revelation of God as a Giver.

Are you giving because of a revelation or merely for a reward? Knowing God as a Giver means knowing why He gives. As I said, money is not provided to us just so we can buy things, such as houses, cars, clothes and other material possessions. Knowing why the Giver gives will enable you to reap successfully. You'll stay focused on the revelation of why God gives. Then when you get money, you won't wander off, doing your own thing with that money God has given you.

You see, some people are sowing money, not because they have the revelation, but because they just want the reward. They don't have the revelation that God gives so they can receive and become a pipeline of financial blessing so that His work can advance. They don't have the revelation of the mission. They can't fulfill the covenant because they can't meet the conditions. They can't put God's work first with their money, because they have their eyes only on the reward. They are thinking about what they are going to be able to buy with more money in their hands.

Reaping according to revelation is a maturing process. You mature in money just as you mature in other areas of life. As you give more and more because you're able to turn loose of your money in faith, God begins to say, *That's it. Turn it loose on him in a full measure. He knows what to do with it. He's not going to turn his back on Me. He's a covenant giver, a money missionary. He's not afraid to turn money loose. He knows I'll get it back to him.*

You see, being a money missionary and doing your part to fulfill the financial covenant is not about rewards and what you're going to get out of it. It's about loving God and wanting to get the job done.

What is your priority? Your financial priority is what God is looking at. Let's look again at the case of a woman whose first priority was the Lord.

> Now when Jesus was in Bethany, in the house of Simon the leper, there came unto him a woman having an alabaster box of very precious ointment, and poured it on his head, as he sat at meat.
>
> But when his disciples saw it, they had indignation, saying, To what purpose is this waste? For this ointment might have been sold for much, and given to the poor.
>
> When Jesus understood it, he said unto them, Why trouble ye the woman? for she hath wrought a GOOD WORK upon me.
>
> Matthew 26:6-10

What was this woman's "good work"? She took something very expensive and put it into Jesus' ministry. Jesus said, ...she hath wrought a good work upon me.

What Will You Give Me?

Let's continue reading this passage to learn more about God's covenant versus the world's covenant.

> **For ye have the poor always with you; but me ye have not always. For in that she hath poured this ointment on my body, she did it for my burial. Verily I say unto you, Wheresoever this gospel shall be preached in the whole world, there shall also this, that this woman hath done, be told for a memorial of her.**
>
> **Then one of the twelve, called Judas Iscariot, went unto the chief priests, and said unto them, WHAT WILL YE GIVE ME, and I will deliver him unto you? And they covenanted with him for thirty pieces of silver.**
>
> **Matthew 26:11-15**

Judas was Jesus' treasurer. He handled money, but he didn't have the revelation. Therefore, he was broke. He had a "broke, gotta-have-more" mentality that ended up ruining him.

Did you know that if you don't get this revelation of money's mission, or purpose, then when you get your paycheck on payday, you will still be broke? You'll always have to worry about money. What economists predict and project will bother you; interest rates will bother you; investment dilemmas will bother you. You will be troubled about money because you will have a "broke" mentality.

When you don't have the assurance that God's hand is on your money, everything will bother you because you will be uncertain of your future. You won't be sure what's going to happen. But once you get the revelation, all the money you have could disappear, and it won't matter to you. You'll know you're in covenant with God, and you'll know that money will be replenished.

God's Financial Covenant Versus the World's Financial Covenant

Look closely at Matthew 26:15: **And [Judas] said unto them** [the chief priests], **WHAT WILL YE GIVE ME, and I will deliver him unto you? And they covenanted with him for thirty pieces of silver.** Notice that phrase "What will ye give me?" That is the world's cry. It is a worldly attitude—"gimme, gimme, gimme."

Christians have been crying out to the world, saying, "What are you going to give me?" For example, someone with a college degree will say, "What are you going to give me for my academics?" And the world answers, "I'm going to give just enough to keep you coming back."

The woman with the alabaster jar wasn't worried about what she was going to get. She wasn't asking, "What will you give me?" No, she went to the Lord with something; she gave what she had to Jesus.

Then there's Judas, the Lord's treasurer, worried about what he's going to get. He said to the chief priests, "What will you give me?"

In a sense, the Church at large is stuck in that rut. They don't understand the mission. People are giving, but they are giving only to receive. Somewhere down the line, they chucked or tossed the love of God out. But to be a money missionary, you have to give because you love Him.

When you have the revelation of the mission and purpose for money, you're not wishy-washy about giving. You give no matter what, because you want to see God's mission accomplished in the earth. I know too much about this, and I know I couldn't live without giving. If there were no such thing as sowing and reaping, I'd still have to give.

We have to get to that place in our attitudes and our thinking if we want to be money missionaries. We can't think of giving as a swap-out deal. If you have that mentality, you are still at the trading post. You are not on the front lines of giving to God as a money missionary.

Now, I'm not saying that it's wrong to expect to receive. We have to expect to receive because the Bible says that we can and should. Faith is still involved in reaping, but faith without works is dead. (James 2:20,26.) In other words, if you're believing for money, but you're not tithing and giving, you're going to come up short in your faith, because you don't have any works. The Word says to tithe and to give, so you can't leave that undone and expect God to pour out His blessings on you financially. Your attitude should be, *I was lost, and somebody told me about Jesus. I want somebody else to hear about Jesus.* Or *I was sick, and somebody laid hands upon me and I was healed. I want somebody else to receive healing too.* Or *I was depressed, and I heard a word from the Lord, and it took*

depression off me. I want somebody else to be released too.
You see, it's not the money—it's the mission.

Judas didn't see it that way. He didn't have the revelation.

But when his disciples saw it, they had indignation, saying, To what purpose is this waste? For this ointment might have been sold for much, and given to the poor.

Matthew 26:8,9

If you read the account of this same incident in John 12:4, you'll find that it was Judas who asked the question, "Why this waste?" Evidently, Judas stirred the other disciples up and no one would rebuke him. Now let's look again at another powerful statement in this passage.

And [Judas] said unto them, What will ye give me, and I will deliver him unto you? And they covenanted with him for thirty pieces of silver.

Matthew 26:15

The last part of this verse says the chief priests covenanted with Judas. We know that Judas did not have the proper revelation of money. He was not on God's system of finances. *And, today, if we are not in covenant with God with our money, we are going to be in covenant with the world.*

A Hard Statement

I know that's a hard statement, but it's true. You are either in covenant with God with your money, or you are in covenant with the world. You may think you're looking to God as your supplier, but you're not. You're looking to the world—you're looking to receive money the way the world receives money. You can't really be looking to God as your source, because, actually, you don't have a right to—you're not in covenant with Him. You could even be tithing, but that doesn't mean you're in covenant with God with your money. If you want a real covenant, you have to be willing to do with your money what He wants you to do. You have to give when He says give.

Look again at Matthew 26:15: **And [Judas] said unto them, What will ye give me, and I will deliver him unto you? And they covenanted with him for thirty pieces of silver.** We know that Judas was not in covenant with God because he was asking the world, "What will you give me?" (Do you know what the world will give you? It will give you a hard way to go and a hard row to hoe!)

As I said, the Church has been at the world's door knocking and ringing the doorbell, trying to qualify for what is already theirs if they'd just stay under the covenant. A born-again person knows that he should not be in debt. He knows that he should have plenty and that His God is bigger than any circumstance of lack.

The Church has been trying to live under the world's covenant. People often quote Hosea 4:6, saying, **My people are destroyed for lack of knowledge.** But let's read that entire verse:

> **My people are destroyed for lack of knowledge:** BECAUSE THOU HAST REJECTED KNOWLEDGE, **I will also reject thee, that thou shalt be no priest to me: seeing thou hast forgotten the law of thy God, I will also forget thy children.**
>
> **Hosea 4:6**

Many have heard the truth and have rejected it. They have money in the bank, but if Jesus, along with Peter, James and John, showed up and asked them for it, they would not give it.

Judas falls into that category of rejecting knowledge. He covenanted with the chief priests to sell Jesus out for thirty pieces of silver. Jesus was a Man who fed 5000 with a little boy's lunch, and summoned a fish to bring Him money for taxes. Judas was too trifling to understand the revelation. How could you have the revelation and sell out such a Man, the Savior?

Had Judas gotten the revelation, that thirty pieces of silver would have been nothing to him compared to what he could have had by following Jesus and serving God and getting into covenant with the Almighty.

Money knows that the earth is the Lord's; money knows to whom it belongs. When money finds people who have a revelation and who know what to do with money, it goes to them.

Someone said, "But money can't think." No, but when you are in covenant with God, He will talk to people who have the money and make sure some of it gets to you.

You see, the devil isn't in control. Certainly, he is the god of this world (2 Cor. 4:4), but when you are in a certain position of having a revelation of money and of being in covenant with God, then God is in control where you are concerned. God will spoil the enemy for you. He did it for His people throughout the Bible, and He does it for His people today.

Friend, you are either in covenant with God, as was the woman who poured the expensive perfume on Jesus' feet, or you are in covenant with the world, as Judas was, and when you get your "thirty pieces of silver," it will always last you just until the next time or just until payday or the first of the month. I encourage you to be one of those of the new breed of men and women who are moving out into a powerful revelation of money and of how to prosper God's way.

You Have To Know the Purpose, or Your Giving Will Seem Like a Waste

As I said before, you can't come into covenant with God fully until you have this revelation, until you know money's purpose. Let's look again at Matthew 26.

Now when Jesus wan in Bethany, in the house of Simon the leper, there came unto him a woman having an alabaster box of very

precious ointment, and poured it on his head,
as he sat at meat.

But when his disciples saw it, they had indignation, saying, To what purpose is this waste?

Matthew 26:6-8

It is obvious from this passage that Judas and the
other disciples did not have the revelation and did not
realize that money's purpose is to be given to the Lord so
He can do with it as He sees fit. You have to know the
real purpose for money, or all your giving will just seem
like a waste. You'll be thinking of other things you could
be using that money for. You won't see the value of
giving—the value of souls being won into the Kingdom—
and you won't see the value of the return, of reaping
God's reward for your obedience.

Again, what is money's purpose? What is God's
money supposed to be used for? The following verse
gives us a clue.

He that committeth sin is of the devil; for
the devil sinneth from the beginning. FOR THIS
PURPOSE the Son of God was manifested, that he
might destroy the works of the devil.

1 John 3:8

When you understand money's mission and you become a money missionary, you are in the process of destroying the works of the devil.

Someone said, "Yes, but Jesus already destroyed the enemy's works." Yes, He did. In His death, burial and resurrection, Jesus defeated Satan. But we have to enforce Satan's defeat in our lives, or he will continue to run roughshod over us. We have to know what Jesus did for us, the price that He paid, and we have to act on that truth for it to set us free (John 8:32), for it to become effectual in our lives. How are people going to know the truth? By hearing it preached. The Bible says, **Faith cometh by hearing, and hearing by the word of God** (Rom. 10:17). Well, how are people going to hear the Word of God? Let's read some more in Romans 10.

> **How then shall they call on him in whom they have not believed? and how shall they believe in him of whom they have not heard? and HOW SHALL THEY HEAR WITHOUT A PREACHER? And how shall they preach, except they be sent? as it is written, How beautiful are the feet of them THAT PREACH THE GOSPEL OF PEACE, and bring glad tidings of good things!**
>
> **Romans 10:14,15**

It takes money to preach the Gospel around the world and to fulfill the covenant mission of harvesting souls for the Kingdom of God. Men and women can't travel, print books or get on the radio or television without money.

The following is an example of a man without a covenant who entered into a covenant with God with his money. In other words, he was a sinner who honored God with his money, and God blessed him and his house as a result.

> **There was a certain man in Caesarea called Cornelius, a centurion of the band called the Italian band, a devout man, and one that feared God with all his house, WHICH GAVE MUCH ALMS TO THE PEOPLE, and prayed to God alway.**
>
> Acts 10:1,2

Here is a man, Cornelius, who does not have a covenant with God. We see later that, although this man was devout, he was unsaved at the time he did his alms-giving and praying. Yet His money moved God.

No, you can't buy salvation, but money can get God's attention when someone is honoring Him with it, as Cornelius did. It doesn't matter if that money is coming from a saved person or a sinner, it gets God's attention if it is put toward His work.

There are some wealthy men today who sometimes "tip" God, and, to a certain degree, God watches over them until they get saved. They are men without a covenant who are honoring God as we see Cornelius doing. Cornelius was a man without a covenant, but his prayer and his money got God's attention and brought him to salvation.

Let's continue reading this passage.

> **He [Cornelius] saw in a vision evidently about the ninth hour of the day an angel of God coming in to him, and saying unto him, Cornelius. And when he looked on him, he was afraid, and said, What is it, Lord? And he said unto him, Thy prayers and thine alms are come up for a memorial before God.**
>
> **Acts 10:3,4**

Because Cornelius was a giver to God's people and to His work, an angel came with a message and called Cornelius by name.

You see, when you open an account with God, so to speak, and make deposits as a money missionary, you have withdrawal rights. When you consistently give and your heart is to do with your money what God says to do, you can make withdrawals on your account. Money will be no problem to you when you stop putting yourself first and begin putting God and His work first.

Consult the Lord in Your Giving

The key to being a money missionary is not just giving; it's giving when God tells you to give and to whom God tells you to give. In other words, you don't need to just give indiscriminately to everyone you meet. But you do need to be willing and obedient when God speaks to you or leads you in a certain direction in your giving.

Ever since God has brought me into my wealthy places, I have been financially able to do certain things for people as I saw their situations, but God doesn't always permit me to meet the need. He told me once, in effect, "Don't try to take My place. You might see situations you could do something about, but you need to consult Me. I might be working something out in their lives. Don't try to take My place and run to their rescue."

You might hear some sad stories about people in
need, but you can't just try to fulfill their needs. So make
sure God told you or led you to give someone money
before you give it. Your money can be dangerous money
when you give out of turn or when you don't give when
you are supposed to. Be careful to consult the Lord. Be
available to Him to put money where He wants you to
put it.

It is God who gives seed to the sower, and it is God
who gives bread to the eater. (Isa. 55:10.) There's nothing
in the world like it when God comes through for you and
meets your need. It's distasteful when people "gouge"
others for something and then talk about what a breakthrough they received. They'll say, "Look what the Lord
did for me!" The Lord didn't do that—they looked to
some man or woman of some means to try to get their
need met that way.

I was sitting in my yard one day reading my Bible
while a man was mowing my yard. He was a substitute
for the fellow who usually took care of my yard. When he
had finished, he walked up to me and asked, "Will you
receive this?" It was a $200 check.

Well, who did that? Certainly, the man gave me the
money. But it was the Lord who prompted him to do it.

And who must then reward this man's giving? The Lord. When God asks you to give, He has a double blessing in mind. He wants to bless the one you give money to, and He wants to bless you in return for your obedience.

So God needs to be the One who's prompting your giving, not some other person or your own feelings. Also, no man should tell you in a service to rush to the altar with your offerings. We've seen it happen time and time again—when the Spirit of God moved in a certain way, people came down to the altar and began giving without anyone prompting them. It was orchestrated by God.

But then men have taken that and have tried to make a ritual out of it. They've tried to bring it down on man's level. (If anyone tells you to rush to the altar, you need to lock your purse up and refuse to give a quarter because God is not in it.)

I preach this message, not to get money for myself, but for the benefit of God's people who will take hold of it and act on it. I don't need money personally, and whether a person gives to my ministry or not does not affect my ministry. It will go on whether a person gives or not. God will finance the vision He gives a minister. And the vision will always be bigger than the money he or she can see; otherwise it wouldn't be a vision. But God will see to it that it's financed. That minister doesn't have to beg or coerce people to finance what God has put in his or her heart.

Let's read Acts 10:1-4 again.

> There was a certain man in Caesarea called Cornelius, a centurion of the band called the Italian band, a devout man, and one that feared God with all his house, which gave much alms to the people, and prayed to God alway.
>
> He saw in a vision evidently about the ninth hour of the day an angel of God coming in to him, and saying unto him, Cornelius. And when he looked on him, he was afraid, and said, What is it, Lord? And he said unto him, Thy prayers and thine alms are come up for a memorial before God.
>
> Acts 10:1-4

Notice that Cornelius was **a devout man, and one that feared God with all his house, WHICH GAVE MUCH ALMS TO THE PEOPLE, and PRAYED TO GOD ALWAY** (v. 2). Notice how prayer goes with giving. Some people want to pray all day, but giving has something to do with it too.

Some people are trying every which way to become prosperous when all the time the Word of God tells them how to do it. I said in a previous chapter that when the mission is understood and put first above everything else, "millionaire status" is released in that person's life. His financial position can become limitless, because you can't out-give God.

But people are trying everything under the sun except what the Word says. I have seen people send money to preachers who were sending out special rags and splashing oil everywhere as gimmicks to try to get people to give. People gave, but they were trying to make a deal. They were distracted from the Word of God by rags and oil. They needed to stay focused.

Usually, gimmicks used to get people to give money will eventually die out, because they aren't built on the Word of God. Jesus said in Matthew 6:33, **But seek ye first the kingdom of God, and his righteousness; and all these things shall be added unto you.** Do you know what He was saying? He was saying, in effect, "Stay focused. Don't let anything distract you from the Kingdom of God and His mission."

Don't let anything distract you from your assignment. Don't keep the phone on the hook, so to speak. Take it off and remain focused on God and His mission. Don't let anyone distract you or rob you of your heritage. You know the Lord is your provider, your source and your deliverer. Your salvation and blessing don't come from a man. So look to the Lord. When He does something, He does it well.

For instance, I know a certain brother in the Lord who was an alcoholic just living on the streets. You could find him lying in a ditch every day. He was forbidden to own a vehicle, because he couldn't stay sober long enough to drive it. But this man had a praying sister. She literally prayed him out of the ditch! And now he's a real man, a man of God. He's clean and sober, and he walks around with his head held high.

The God I serve delivered that man. And the God I serve wants to deliver others who are held fast by the chains of sin. When God delivers people of the mess they're in, they know it was God who did it, not some man.

Increase and Honor or Decrease and Shame?

Similarly, you know who has brought you up to where you are today financially compared to where you were in years past. God did it, so quit looking to the world for answers. Being in covenant with God brings increase and honor. Being in covenant with the world brings decrease and shame.

We've been talking about one aspect of that covenant, and that is to put His mission first. But the covenant is twofold. God will fulfill His part of the covenant too. Because you are in covenant with God, He has to show Himself strong on your behalf that the heathen might know that your God is bigger than their god. When you are fulfilling your part of the covenant, God must rise up in the midst of your obedience and show the heathen around you that God is in the town where you live. God is living in your house, showing Himself strong on your behalf!

God royally takes care of His own when they obey Him so that the heathen might know that the true and living God is bigger than their god. We need to be able to tell the heathen, "My God is bigger than your god." How can we tell them? How can we show them? One way is by being out of debt and by living in the best, driving the best and wearing the best. Remember, the Lord said in Isaiah 1:19, **If ye be willing and obedient, ye shall eat**

the good of the land. One translation says, "You shall eat the best the land has to offer."

A well-known minister recently shared something with me. He said that the word "recompense" in the Bible connotes money on its feet headed toward. When you give to God, money gets on its feet and starts heading toward you!

Someone said, "I didn't know money could walk." Well, Luke 6:38 says, **Give, and it shall be given unto you; good measure, pressed down, and shaken together, and running over, shall men give into your bosom. For with the same measure that ye mete withal it shall be measured to you again.** Money walks through men's hands. That's how God is going to get money to you—through the hands of men.

You can enter into a covenant with God by becoming a money missionary. By doing that, you will be putting your finances under the anointing. Be careful not to contaminate that anointing with your mouth by talking against people or by speaking words of unbelief. With your finances under the anointing, increase must come your way. Money will have to turn in your direction and head your way. Men will bring money to you. So just stay under that anointing where God by His Spirit can rearrange things for you financially and set you in a sure place. When you use your money for God's mission, God will bring you into your wealthy place. Confess this and mean it in your heart: "I'm headed to my wealthy place because I'm using my wealth for God's mission. I'm fulfilling my part of the covenant, and I'll never be broke another day in my life. In fact, I'm going to prosper all the days of my life. Money cometh to me now!"

In the previous chapters of this book, I have briefly mentioned the anointing that is released when you become a money missionary and possess the revelation of money's real purpose—to finance the Lord's mission. That anointing is released after you do something. In other words, it's not automatic. But when that anointing is released (remember, I called it "millionaire status"), the application of that anointing is twofold.

First, the money you sow will be used to preach the Gospel, whereby burdens can be removed and yokes destroyed from the hearers. (Isa. 10:27.)

Second, when you sow money in obedience to God, that burden-removing, yoke-destroying anointing begins to rest on your finances. You enter into a covenant with God that cannot be broken as long as you are obeying Him.

When God told me to have people confess, "I'll never be broke another day in my life!" He told me that those words were anointed and explosive and that power was contained in those words. There is power in those words to change things in a person's life. That's why I exhort people to seek God's face for wisdom and understanding of the meaning of the things He has revealed so that the words don't become just a good saying or a cliché. With revelation comes the anointing to carry out or to fulfill the revelation when it is acted on in faith. In other words, whatever the Spirit of God says is yours you can claim by faith as yours now!

God Gave Us the Works!

God has given us many things, including a commission to preach the Gospel around the world. In an earlier chapter, we talked about doing the works of Jesus (and that includes financing the works of Jesus) in connection with fulfilling a covenant. Let's study further this important verse in John 14.

> **Verily, verily, I say unto you, He that elieveth on me, THE WORKS that I do shall he do**

also; and greater works than these shall he do; because I go unto my Father.

John 14:12

I want you to think about two things when you see "the works." I want you to think about the anointing and finances. God has given us "the works" to do, but He knows we have to have money to do the works. Therefore, along with the anointing to do the works, the finances have been provided for us too!

As I said in a previous chapter, the greater works that Jesus speaks about in this verse cannot be talking about greater works in quality, because the works that Jesus did, He did by the Spirit of God, and Jesus had the Spirit without measure. (John 3:34.) The works of Jesus that we do, we also do by the Spirit of God, but individually, we only have the Spirit in a measure. Therefore, Jesus is talking about a greater *quantity* of works, not a greater *quality* of works.

If the quantity level of anything rises, it takes more volume to take care of it. Concerning the greater works of Jesus, it is going to take a greater volume of people, of manpower, to take care of it, and it is going to take a greater volume of money to accomplish it. When we give

money to God's work—putting Him first in our giving—
our money magnifies the Lord's work.

What exactly are the works that God has anointed us
and provided for us financially to do? Read carefully the
following passages of Scripture.

> **The Spirit of the Lord is upon me [Jesus],
> because he hath anointed me to preach the
> gospel to the poor; he hath sent me to heal the
> brokenhearted, to preach deliverance to the
> captives, and recovering of sight to the blind, to
> set at liberty them that are bruised, to preach
> the acceptable year of the Lord.**
>
> **Luke 4:18,19**

> **And Jesus came and spoke unto them,
> saying, All power is given unto me in heaven
> and in earth.**
>
> **Go ye therefore, and teach all nations,
> baptizing them in the name of the Father, and
> of the Son, and of the Holy Ghost: teaching
> them to observe all things whatsoever I have
> commanded you: and, lo, I am with you alway,
> even unto the end of the world. Amen.**

Matthew 28:18-20

And he said unto them, Go ye into all the
world, and preach the gospel to every creature.
He that believeth and is baptized shall be saved;
but he that believeth not shall be damned. And
these signs shall follow them that believe; In my
name shall they cast out devils; they shall speak
with new tongues; they shall take up serpents;
and if they drink any deadly thing, it shall not
hurt them; they shall lay hands on the sick, and
they shall recover.

Mark 16:15-18

Our accomplishing God's work on the earth is the
very thing that is going to usher in the return of Jesus
Christ. Jesus is waiting on one mission to be accomplished, and we just read about the mission—the preaching of the Gospel around the world with signs and
wonders following.

Let's continue reading in Mark 16.

So then after the Lord had spoken unto
them, he was received up into heaven, and sat
on the right hand of God.

And they went forth, and preached EVERY WHERE, the Lord working with them, and confirming the word with signs following. Amen.

Mark 16:19,20

Notice the statement **they went forth, and preached every where** (v. 20). In order to do that, they had to have financing, Holy Ghost financing, as well as Holy Ghost anointing.

If you will, the Church acts as a liaison between Heaven and earth to fulfill God's plan and purpose on the earth. We are carrying out God's orders. Well, since God's orders are to preach the Gospel and do the greater works, then His orders must include using our money to see that it is done. Have you been able to travel the globe lately for free? No, you haven't and neither can the men and women who answer God's call as missionaries and evangelists to travel the globe with the Gospel. It takes money to do the work.

Some people act wounded and offended if you teach about money in connection with the anointing. In fact, they don't want to hear money talked about in church at all. You would think they are against prosperity, but then they have no problem wanting a raise at their job! I don't

know why they'd want a raise if they were against prosperity. They should go ahead and work for nothing!

If every Christian would tithe, we could do so much
more than we've been able to do. But beyond the tithe,
we need to be giving offerings, too, so that men and
women can do all that the Lord is telling them to do.

Some Christians own prosperous businesses and yet
don't tithe. I know personally of one businesswoman
who resisted tithing until she was figuring her earnings
one time and came up $30,000 short. Putting into
practice Malachi 3:10-11 could have solved this
woman's problem.

> **Bring ye all the tithes into the storehouse,**
> **that there may be meat in mine house, and**
> **prove me now herewith, saith the Lord of hosts,**
> **if I will not open you the windows of heaven,**
> **and pour you out a blessing, that there shall not**
> **be room enough to receive it.**

> **And I will rebuke the devourer for your sakes,**
> **and he shall not destroy the fruits of your ground;**
> **neither shall your vine cast her fruit before the**
> **time in the field, saith the Lord of hosts.**

Well, it wasn't that God *wouldn't* rebuke the devourer from this woman's business; He *couldn't* do it, because she was not cooperating with Him in obedience to His Word. And she couldn't take authority over the devourer, either. She couldn't claim any "tither's rights," because she wasn't tithing.

This woman later told me, "I'm paying tithes from now on. There's no way I'm going to miss paying them."

We need to take seriously what God's Word says about giving and receiving. We need to listen to and take seriously this message of money with a mission. Money with a mission is money that magnifies the Lord's work. God is going to use us as channels to do the greater works, whether or not we go to Africa, America, Asia, Australia or Europe as full-time ministers of the Gospel. Certainly, we are called to minister and to be witnesses in our own communities, but even if one is not called personally to herald the Gospel around the world, he or she can send others. Remember, I said that every child of God is a money missionary.

Magnifying the Lord's work can only come through your anointed giving—through your understanding God's mission and money's purpose and then giving money accordingly in obedience to Him. But there are different aspects of magnifying the Lord's work that I want to look at.

> **Let them shout for joy, and be glad, that favour my righteous cause: yea, let them say continually, LET THE LORD BE MAGNIFIED, which hath pleasure in the prosperity of his servant.**
>
> **Psalm 35:27**

The Lord takes pleasure in your prosperity. He is magnified when His people prosper His way—when they allow Him to take them into their wealthy places through their obedience to Him. Some Christians have been trying to magnify God to the world, but they are broke, impoverished, and beaten down. They are trying to win the world, but the only thing many in the world understand is money. They don't understand speaking in tongues, getting "drunk" in the Spirit or falling out under the power of God. But when they see someone full of the Holy Ghost dressing right, driving right, living right and loving Jesus, that gets their attention.

Anointed Prosperity Is a Result of Anointed Giving

Some people in the world will snub you if you're broke. You wouldn't be able to get them to listen to you. But when you start magnifying the Lord's work through anointed giving, you'll begin living in anointed prosperity, and those people will have ears to hear what you are saying. The door will be opened to you to preach the Gospel to them.

Someone said, "Well, it's not right to snub someone just because he's not rich." No, it's not, but sinners who do that don't usually mean any harm; they just don't know any better.

Let's read Psalm 35:27 again and look at a different aspect of magnifying the Lord with our money.

> **Let them shout for joy, and be glad, that favour my righteous cause: yea, let them say continually, Let the Lord be magnified, which hath pleasure in the prosperity of his servant.**

Notice that the words "joy" and "glad" are used in the same verse. The Holy Ghost is saying that a person can be full of joy and gladness when he does a certain thing. When he does what? When he favors God's righteous cause. What is "favoring God's righteous cause"? It's favoring the mission. How do you favor the mission? You do it with your money.

Now the pleasure that God has in the prosperity of His servants is not only in the fact that they have stuff, but in the fact that His work will flourish around the world because they are favoring His righteous cause. In other words, they are not getting prosperity and then sitting on it, hiding it from the Lord. No, they are planting it into His Kingdom so that the work will go unhindered.

As I said, the mission is more than about your house, your car, your new clothes and your fancy shoes and hair-dos. It is about covenant. It's about favoring God's cause. Some people are more concerned about their hair-dos than they are about the covenant. Many are more concerned about their houses than they are about the Lord's house.

I was ministering this message once, and the Lord inspired me to say the following, talking about what He's done for man:

> *I am the Lord, who took you out of the outhouse*
> *and built the inside bathroom for you. I am the One*

who took you out of the cold. I took you from warming yourself by the fireplace, where you were hot in the front and cold in the back. I put you in central heating. I am the One. I took the black man off the plantation as a slave when men were whipping him and treating him like an animal. I released the black man from being a slave and the white man from being a slave-driver. Everybody went free. And you mean to tell Me that you are going to turn your back on My work? I brought you such a long way. I brought the illiterate out when he couldn't read. I did it by My grace.

I brought you out when no one could bring you out. When no one else wanted you, I wanted you. I took you in. I nourished and nurtured you like a hen nurses her chicks. I wiped the tears from your grandmother's eyes. I saw your future and the day that you would be free to declare My name. Don't you back up now. Come forward and take your rightful place. I am the Lord thy God, who put My hand on you when you couldn't do anything for yourself. I brought you through school, from grade school to college. When you didn't have the money to pay tuition or make your house payment, I saw to it that your need was met.

Your Mama and your Daddy didn't do it. I made a way for you.

I am the One who opened up that job for you when no one else wanted to hire you. I am El Shaddai. I am Jehovah Jireh—I am your Provider. You may look as if you are going under, but I am not going to let you go under. I have a solid foundation under you. My Word is a solid rock, so stand on My Word.

You have a place to lay your head, and your needs are met. Some have houses, fancy cars and the finest clothes. Remember, I am the One who brought you out and brought you up. I am the One who brings you through seen and unseen danger. If the enemy could have done it, he would have taken you out by now. But I am holding you; I have some work for you to do. I have some people I want you to preach to. I have some people I want you to pray for. I have some people who need to hear My name. Didn't I tell you that in My name you would cast out devils and lay hands on the sick? I am the One who brought you out and who called and commissioned you. Don't turn away from Me. Sell out to Me completely. I am the Lord.

The Principle and the Purpose

Many believers have gotten so caught up in the principles of financial increase that they have lost sight of the purpose for financial increase. They have gotten hold of the fact that they need to release their finances by giving willingly, cheerfully and obediently to the Lord's work. But they have forgotten the purpose for their giving.

Purpose, Principle, Power and Provision

You can understand a principle, but if you don't understand the purpose, you are not going to work the principle properly. You will just be going through the motions. We've learned a lot of principles in the Charismatic movement, but when we unite principles with an understanding of the purpose, power comes on the scene to bring provision!

Also, when you understand the purpose, you have the passion to stick with the principle. Then when some broke, unlearned, ignorant brother or sister with a "grasshopper mentality" (Num. 13:33) comes along to try to talk you out of the provision, the power will still be there because of the passion. You'll know in your heart the right thing to do, and no one will be able to talk you out of it.

Some people want to accuse me, saying, "All you talk about is money." Well, I'm going to talk about it until it starts showing up in more people's lives. Then I'll change my conversation! I tell you, too many have a grasshopper mentality. Bills and debts have loomed over their heads like "Goliaths," but there is a new breed of Christians who've gone down to the brook to pick up some stones. They are going to face those Goliaths head-on and put them in their place!

See Your Seed as Precious

Some people want to be money missionaries, but they are not esteeming what they have for God to work with. They say, "Well, I'd give if I had more. But I don't have much. What does the Lord need with my little bit?"

I want you to see that it's not how much money you have, but what that money is for. What is your money for? If it's for the Lord, consider what you have to give as precious seed, because God can multiply it for His use and multiply it some more to give back to you.

Let's read a biblical example of that very thing happening. I'm talking about the little boy with five loaves and two fishes. We can read about it in Matthew, Mark, Luke and John, but I'm going to share first from Matthew's account.

> And when it was evening, his disciples came to him, saying, This is a desert place, and the time is now past; send the multitude away, that they may go into the villages, and buy themselves victuals.
>
> But Jesus said unto them, They need not depart; give ye them to eat.
>
> And they say unto him, We have here but five loaves, and two fishes.
>
> He said, Bring them hither to me. And he commanded the multitude to sit down on the grass, and took THE FIVE LOAVES, AND THE TWO FISHES, and looking up to heaven, he blessed, and brake, and gave the loaves to his disciples, and the disciples to the multitude. AND THEY DID

ALL EAT, AND WERE FILLED: **and they took up of the fragments that remained twelve baskets full. And they that had eaten were about five thousand men, beside women and children.**

Matthew 14:15-21

John's account says,

When Jesus then lifted up his eyes, and saw a great company come unto him, he saith unto Philip, Whence shall we buy bread, that these may eat?

[Philip answered,] There is a lad here, which hath five barley loaves, and two small fishes: but what are they among so many?

John 6:5,9

When you understand what the Lord did with that little boy's seed—his five loaves and two fishes—you will understand that your money, no matter how much it is, is precious because it can "explode" and be multiplied at any minute when you give it to the Lord.

So if God gives you an assignment with two dollars, shout, because that two dollars can turn out to be anything God wants it to be. That two dollars is precious seed, and you need to see it that way.

You see, every one of your dollars becomes precious when it is stamped with the anointing. When your money is put toward a mission, it is stamped with the anointing, and that anointing can cause abundance at any second. That little boy's lunch became seed for Almighty God's mission, and the anointing came on those few loaves and fishes and "exploded" them into a harvest for those 5000 men. Then after everyone ate, it was as if God said, "I'm going to give that boy more fish and more bread."

> **And they did all eat, and were filled: and**
> **THEY TOOK UP OF THE FRAGMENTS THAT REMAINED**
> **TWELVE BASKETS FULL.**
>
> **Matthew 14:20**

I mean, that boy went home with some bread!

I bet that because that boy knew the system, he didn't actually take all of those baskets home for himself and his family. I can just imagine him stopping by house after house, visiting families who needed food. I think that boy became a "money missionary" and began to supply the needs of God's people as he traveled home.

When God gives you a harvest, or a return on your giving, don't run home with your baskets. Why try to keep all that bread when you can have the whole bakery if you stay on God's system?

We need to esteem the seed that God gives us and see it as precious, not so we can hold on tight to it, but so that we can use it for God's purpose. In previous chapters, I mentioned the woman with the alabaster box who poured that expensive perfume on Jesus. The Bible says the perfume, or ointment, was very precious. (Matt. 26:7.) It was precious, but it didn't mean more to her than Jesus did. She got in on the mission. She didn't hold anything back. She poured out that ointment. (Notice she poured it out—she didn't measure it out.)

Similarly, when you are ready to give Jesus your all, including your money, then you will become a money missionary, and you will be ready to receive an abundant harvest. You won't be looking for more barns or places to store and hoard your harvest. Instead, you'll be looking to plant more into the Kingdom of God.

To be a money missionary, you have to be like that woman; she took something valuable and precious and poured it all out to Jesus. She didn't care how much it cost.

Are you ready to pour out of your substance where He tells you to pour it and when He tells you to do it? When you pour out of your finances unto God, as we have seen, it sets up a memorial in the mind of God, a memorial of your faithfulness and love for Him.

Let's look again at the disciples' reaction to this woman's act of faithfulness.

But when his disciples saw it, they had indignation, saying, To what purpose is this waste?
Matthew 26:8

The disciples did not understand the purpose, and when you don't understand the purpose, you can get into trouble. You remember what God said to Abraham:

And I will bless them that bless thee, and curse him that curseth thee: and in thee shall all families of the earth be blessed.
Genesis 12:3

When you don't understand the purpose, you could say things against those who do understand the purpose, and end up cursing yourself. Then you might try to speak blessing over your life, but the curse is overriding the blessing.

Just a Waste of Money

As I said before, when you don't have a revelation in your heart of the purpose, you will see giving as just a waste of money. I plan to build one of the most beautiful sanctuaries in the state of Louisiana. But when I do, I'm sure there will be some who will walk through the front doors into the foyer and say, "They didn't need to do all this. This is a waste of money." But if you'll remember, Solomon's temple, which was built for and dedicated to the Lord, was resplendent with beauty.

Anything that glorifies and magnifies God is not a waste. But if you don't have a revelation of money's purpose and of God's mission, and you call giving a waste, then that revelation will not come to you, because you have no appreciation for giving. If money did come to you, you would not know or acknowledge that it came from God. You would think you got it by your own talent and strength.

God has revealed to us money's purpose for a reason. The reason is to keep us in check where money is concerned and to ensure that His work will go on. When you resist the reason, you hold yourself back from going any further in divine prosperity.

In Matthew 26:8, the disciples wanted to know the purpose for "this waste," talking about the woman's pouring out her expensive perfume on Jesus. They were not magnifying the Lord or His work with their money, and they didn't want anyone else to magnify the Lord, either.

> **For this ointment might have been sold for much, and given to the poor.**
>
> **Matthew 26:9**

The disciples were concerned about making a dollar. They were thinking about a natural means of getting money, while the woman was tapping into supernatural prosperity. Today, we want to sell everything instead of giving something. But if you give, God can multiply it. He can multiply your seed sown.

The disciples were thinking about a business transaction while, right under their noses, this woman was making a supernatural transaction. They had no revelation. If you don't have a revelation, a supernatural transaction could be happening before your eyes, and you will miss it. You won't see it.

The disciples wanted to sell that perfume, but that girl beat them to it. She gave it away instead. God's system is not a selling system. The principle of seedtime and harvest doesn't work if you're selling when you should be giving. Seedtime and harvest is about giving.

If the disciples had sold that perfume, they only would have received a certain amount one time, and that would have been the end of it. But the woman created a memorial and got under the anointing whereby divine prosperity could come to her.

In the denomination I came out of, we tried to sell things to take the place of our tithing. It was a trick of the devil to keep us broke. No matter how much we sold, we were still broke or just barely getting by, struggling. Why? Because there was no dividend or return happening. Nothing was coming back to us on what we sold except what we got right there on the spot. We were selling a lot of fried chicken and fish dinners, and the devil kept us broke and unable to get the Gospel out as we should have.

But, bless God, I've got good news for you. We are not selling the chicken anymore; we are eating the chicken. We are not selling the fish anymore; we are eating the fish. We are tithing and planting our money into the Kingdom by giving offerings, and supernatural favor and financial progress is coming our way to wipe out every kind of money problem we've ever had! This is our hour! But we have to have a revelation.

Become Seed-Minded, Not Selling-Minded

Prosperity is not about money; it's about the mission. But it takes money to carry out the mission. And we're not going to get the money by selling things and making deals. I tell you, I don't believe in garage sales. Some people want to have a garage sale and sell their things to get rid of them when they should be giving those things away. You might make $200 from a garage sale, but by giving those things away instead of selling them, you could be setting yourself up for millionaire status to be released. You could become more prosperous than you ever thought possible over that one garage giveaway! Why? Because what you give is your seed. And your seed sown is what God multiplies and gives back to you.

Become seed-minded, not selling-minded. It's your giving that magnifies the Lord's work, not your selling things and making deals. Do you remember the story I told earlier about giving away my car? I know if I had not given that woman my car in obedience to the Lord, I wouldn't be driving what I drive today. It wasn't the size of the car I gave her or even the kind of car I gave her. The Lord said, *She needs a ride.* I obeyed God, and it became a memorial in God's mind.

Payday doesn't always come every Friday in seedtime and harvest, but it always comes when you're sowing in faith. Harvest always follows seedtime at some point, if you're faithful. Ecclesiastes 11:1 says, **Cast thy bread upon the waters: for thou shalt find it after many days.**

You might not know how many days. That's why you have to keep sowing every time the Lord tells you to sow. Then, finally, you're going to hit a deposit; Jesus is going to stand up and say, "Father, I think that's enough. We need to do something for him. He's obeyed you stead-fastly. I'm standing on his behalf."

When Stephen was being martyred, the book of Acts says, **But he** [Stephen], **being full of the Holy Ghost, looked up stedfastly into heaven, and saw the glory of God, and Jesus standing on the right hand of God** (Act. 7:55). Our steadfastness gets Jesus on His feet! Jesus stands when we are steadfastly doing what He told us to do. And when Jesus stands for us, we receive great reward both here and in Heaven.

I tell you, this thing is settled forever. God's Word cannot fail you, but you have to have some understanding as to how to work the Word. One thing you must do is settle in your heart that God's Word is forever settled. (Ps. 119:89.) Become fully persuaded (Rom. 4:21.)

Another thing you must do is cast down every imagination and argument and reasoning that is contrary to the Word. (2 Cor. 10:5.) When thoughts come that the Word is not going to work for you, say, "I'm not going to believe that. I'm not going to accept that. I cast that down. I'm working on something, and I'm on my way. I don't have time for doubt."

Make up your mind that God's Word is true, that you have a covenant with Him, and that you'll never be broke another day in your life. Make up your mind that your "broke" days are over. Then say what you mean, and mean from your heart what you say. Confess continually, "I'll never be broke another day in my life." That means you're going to have to stay in the Word continually. It's not a one-time shot. In other words, you can't just read a few Scriptures once and make this kind of a confession.

The Mission: Possible

Revelation knowledge knocks the devil out, so to speak. He has lied to Christians for so long that money is evil, and many have been afraid of money. If you have had some hang-ups about money, just shift over to the mission. In other words, when you are having problems in your mind over money, just tell the Lord, "I'm willing to fulfill the mission." Every time negative thoughts come, just say, "Mission." Remind yourself that God's mission needs to be accomplished and that it is possible that you be a part of accomplishing it.

It is possible for you to be a money missionary and be a big giver. It's possible for you to be out of debt. It's possible for you to have more than enough. It's possible!

Money's Other Purpose

Your money is mission money. Therefore, you need to have plenty of it. So far, we've talked about the mission and about money's purpose. But there's more to the purpose than we've covered. Money's purpose is to herald the Gospel and to do the greater works, but there's more to it. Money's purpose is also to show folks that our heavenly Father is a good Father, and He takes care of His children well.

Now, many have a problem with that, but it's true anyway. God wants to show Himself strong in the earth realm in every facet of His children's lives. That includes the houses they live in, the cars they drive, the clothes they wear, the food they eat and so forth. Whatever the best is, you should have it. God has no problem with seeing that you get it. If He did, He messed up with Abraham by making him exceedingly rich. If God had a problem with man's prosperity, He also messed up with Isaac, Jacob and the rest of the Old Testament men and women who had a covenant with Him.

God wants the world to acknowledge the fact that you are blessed because of Him.

> **And their seed shall be known among the Gentiles, and their offspring among the people:** ALL THAT SEE THEM SHALL ACKNOWLEDGE **them,** THAT THEY ARE THE SEED WHICH THE LORD HATH BLESSED.
>
> **Isaiah 61:9**

One translation says, **...as they see them walk in their prosperity.** That's powerful. God does not want you hiding your blessing. When He blesses you, He doesn't intend for you to hide it under a bushel, so to speak.

Some people feel guilty about receiving their heart's desires, but God does grant the desires of your heart. (Ps. 37:4.) He has given me my heart's desires, but I put them in their place by honoring Him first and by being a money missionary.

I know of ministers who hide what God blesses them with. They are afraid for some reason or another. But as long as they are doing what they are supposed to be doing, no one can bother them. People may talk about them, but that talking isn't going to hurt anyone except the people who are doing it.

Don't ever hide your blessing. Have the right relationship with material things, and then openly glorify and magnify God. (I always say, "Drive your blessing out in the open and park it under a light so God can get the glory"!)

> **And it shall come to pass, if thou shalt hearken diligently unto the voice of the Lord thy God, to observe and to do all his commandments which I command thee this day, that the Lord thy God will seat thee on high above all**

nations of the earth: and all these blessings
shall come on thee, and overtake thee, if thou
shalt hearken unto the voice of the Lord thy
God.

Blessed [or empowered to prosper] shalt thou
be IN THE CITY, and blessed shalt thou be IN THE
FIELD.

Deuteronomy 28:1-3

I have some minister friends who are from big cities.
They've learned to walk in divine prosperity, and they are
walking in it big. But they know I have it going on
because I'm not from a big city. I'm in the field! But
when I get around these city boys, we all look alike,
because God said, *I'll bless you in the city, and I'll bless you
in the field.*

And when those city boys come to my house, they
don't know that they're not in the city. I have a city house
in the field! But God gave it to me; it is a house that
glorifies Him. And it's paid for. Through the revelation of
prosperity that God gave to me, my wife and I have paid
off a thirty-year mortgage in five years.

Now let's read another verse of Deuteronomy 28. This is the part I want you to see concerning money's other purpose.

> **And all people of the earth shall SEE that thou art called by the name of the Lord; and they shall be afraid of thee.**
>
> **Deuteronomy 28:10**

People are supposed to see that God's hand is upon the Christian—and not just spiritually. People are supposed to see that God's people are financially blessed. But there aren't too many in that category who are astounding the world. It's not crowded in that category! And if you're in that category, some people, even fellow-believers, look at you like you're going the wrong way.

Someone said, "We've been going this way for so long." Well, it's time to turn around and go the Bible way. It's time to stop thinking prayer is going to do it. No, we need to stop praying and start shouting, saying, "The Lord is here! We are blessed!" Deuteronomy 28:10 says, **And ALL people of the earth shall see....** That means good folks, bad folks, folks who like you and folks who don't like you. It means black folks, white folks and folks of all colors. All people are supposed to see that you are blessed!

> And the Lord shall make thee plenteous in goods, in the fruit of thy body, and in the fruit of thy cattle, and in the fruit of thy ground, in the land which the Lord sware unto thy fathers to give thee.
>
> The Lord [Himself] shall OPEN UNTO THEE HIS GOOD TREASURE, the heaven to give the rain unto thy land in his season, and to bless all the work of thine hand: and thou shalt lend unto many nations, and thou shalt not borrow.
>
> Deuteronomy 28:11,12

Notice verse 12: **The Lord shall open unto thee his good treasure....** In another place, the Bible says, **the Lord himself shall descend from heaven with a shout, with the voice of the archangel, and with the trump of God: and the dead in Christ shall rise first** (1 Thess. 4:16). Notice it says, THE LORD HIMSELF shall descend....

You see, there are some things the Lord doesn't send anyone else to do. And as much as He Himself is going to get those people out of the grave (**...the dead in Christ**

shall rise first), He Himself is going to open unto you His good treasure. (Deut. 28:12.) The same Lord who is going to descend with a shout and open the graves of all those people is going to open unto us His good treasure! But He wants to do it for us now, before we go to our graves!

Let's continue reading this passage in Deuteronomy 28.

> **And the Lord shall make thee the head, and not the tail; and thou shalt be above only, and thou shalt not be beneath; if that thou hearken unto the commandments of the Lord thy God, which I command thee this day, to observe and to do them.**
>
> **Deuteronomy 28:13**

We are the head, not the tail. I can tell you from experience that it's rough back there being the tail. But I am the head now, glory to God. I have a good wife, good children, a happy, healthy family, a successful ministry, plenty of money and so forth. And I'm not hiding it, because we just read that God wants these things to be seen.

As I said before, some ministers want to hide what the Lord has done for them, as if they are afraid of what others might think. But God didn't give them the things they have so they could hide them. He gave them to let all of His children know that He can and will do what He said He would do when we are faithful to His mission. When we use our money to magnify His work, He wants to turn around and magnify us in the world's eyes.

Are you being faithful to the mission? If you are, then what the Lord has done for me, He wants to do for you. But if you don't see it happening in the lives of others because they are hiding their blessing and refusing to testify, you won't have a clear, tangible vision of what the Lord wants to do for you.

"Not Beneath"—That's Talking About Money!

Let's look at the second part of Deuteronomy 28:13, which talks about our being on top and not on the bottom.

...and thou shalt be above only, and thou shalt not be beneath; if that thou hearken unto the commandments of the Lord thy God,

**which I command thee this day, to observe
and to do them.**

First, this verse said, **The Lord shall make thee the
head, and not the tail....** Then, as if that weren't enough,
the Lord repeated Himself right after that: **...and thou
shalt be above only, and thou shalt not be beneath....**
There should be no doubt as to the Lord's will. He wants
us to be "the head," and He wants us to be "above only."

"Yes," someone said, "but how do we know that's
talking about money?" If you read this verse in context,
what else could you conclude that He's talking about?
When God said in verse 3, **Blessed shalt thou be in the
city, and blessed shalt thou be in the field,** do you
think He was talking about having two billy goats? No,
this passage is talking about material, financial abundance—about having more than enough.

Magnifying the Lord

We can't magnify a covenant God by being broke,
poor and barely making it. We can't talk about His love
and care and provision while never appropriating and
operating in His blessing ourselves. We need to magnify
the Lord by using our money for the mission and by

cooperating with Him so that He can multiply money back to us and bring us out of every financial problem and into divine wealth.

Our money can magnify the Lord and His work if we are using it properly. First, it can pave the way for the Gospel to be preached and the greater works to be wrought. Second, it can show the world that God cares for His own.

Let's look at money in a different light than we've been seeing it. Let's see it as money with a purpose, a divine assignment, a mission. Let's become money missionaries for the Lord and see what He will do in the earth—both in bringing in a great harvest of souls and in prospering His children in ways they have not known before.

About the Author

Dr. Leroy Thompson Sr. is the pastor and founder of Word of Life Christian Center in Darrow, Louisiana, a growing and thriving body of believers from various walks of life. He has been in the ministry for twenty-two years, serving for twenty years as a pastor. Even though he completed his undergraduate degree and theology doctorate and was an instructor for several years at a Christian Bible college in Louisiana, it wasn't until 1983, when he received the baptism in the Holy Spirit, that the revelation knowledge of God's Word changed his life; and it continues to increase his ministry. Dr. Thompson attributes the success of his life and ministry to his reliance on the Word of God, being filled with the Holy Spirit and being led by the Spirit of God. Today Dr. Thompson travels across the United States taking the message of ministerial excellence, dedication and discipline to the Body of Christ.

To contact Dr. Leroy Thompson Sr.

write:

Dr. Leroy Thompson Sr.

Ever Increasing Word Ministries

P.O. Box 7

Darrow, Louisiana 70725

Please include your prayer requests

and comments when you write.

Other Books by Dr. Leroy Thompson Sr.

What To Do When Your Faith Is Challenged

The Voice of Jesus—Speaking God's Word With Authority

Available from your local bookstore.

HARRISON HOUSE
Tulsa, Oklahoma 74153

The Harrison House Vision

Proclaiming the truth and the power

Of the Gospel of Jesus Christ

With excellence;

Challenging Christians to

Live victoriously,

Grow spiritually,

Know God intimately.

LEGACY USA
ASK THE DOCTOR
ARRit